The Princeton Review

Word Smart
Genius Edition

How to Build an Erudite Vocabulary

Books in The Princeton Review Series

Cracking the ACT
Cracking the ACT with Sample Tests on Computer Disk
Cracking the GED
Cracking the GMAT
Cracking the GMAT with Sample Tests on Computer Disk
Cracking the GRE
Cracking the GRE with Sample Tests on Computer Disk
Cracking the GRE Psychology Subject Test
Cracking the LSAT
Cracking the LSAT with Sample Tests on Computer Disk
Cracking the MCAT
Cracking the MCAT with Sample Tests on Computer Disk
Cracking the SAT and PSAT
Cracking the SAT and PSAT with Sample Tests on Computer Disk
Cracking the SAT II: Biology Subject Test
Cracking the SAT II: Chemistry Subject Test
Cracking the SAT II: English Subject Tests
Cracking the SAT II: French Subject Test
Cracking the SAT II: History Subject Tests
Cracking the SAT II: Math Subject Tests
Cracking the SAT II: Physics Subject Test
Cracking the SAT II: Spanish Subject Test
Cracking the TOEFL with Audiocassette

SAT Math Workout
SAT Verbal Workout

Don't Be a Chump!
How to Survive Without Your Parents' Money
Trashproof Resumes

Grammar Smart
Math Smart
Reading Smart
Study Smart
Word Smart: Building an Educated Vocabulary
Word Smart II: How to Build a More Educated Vocabulary
Word Smart Executive Edition: Words for Suits
Word Smart Genius: How to Build an Erudite Vocabulary
Writing Smart

Grammar Smart Junior
Math Smart Junior
Word Smart Junior
Writing Smart Junior

Student Access Guide to America's Top Internships
Student Access Guide to College Admissions
Student Access Guide to the Best Business Schools
Student Access Guide to the Best Law Schools
Student Access Guide to the Best Medical Schools
Student Access Guide to the Best 309 Colleges
Student Access Guide to Paying for College
Student Access Guide to Visiting College Campuses
Student Access Guide: The Big Book of Colleges
Student Access Guide: The Internship Bible

Also available on cassette from Living Language

Grammar Smart
Word Smart
Word Smart II

The Princeton Review

Word Smart
Genius Edition

How to Build an Erudite Vocabulary

by Michael Freedman

Random House, Inc., New York 1995

ISBN   0-679-76457-7

ACKNOWLEDGMENTS

The author would like to especially thank his wife Grace and his son Jacob. He would also like to thank Chris Kensler, Susan Cohen, Lee Elliott, Alex Costley, Chris Scott, Illeny Maaza, and Meher Khambata for their editorial and production expertise.

CONTENTS

INTRODUCTION

WHY SHOULD THE SMART HAVE TO SUFFER?

If you already possess a strong vocabulary, you may find most vocabulary books useless—the words are either too easy or they are so obscure that you will never have any use for them. It seems that authors of other books on the market are primarily concerned with weird words that are only useful for party conversations.

To improve your vocabulary, you need to learn words that are used in magazines, novels, and newspapers. The best way to do this is to look up words that you don't know as you find them in your reading. Unfortunately, only the most conscientious of us actually get up out of our chair to find a dictionary. Sometimes we don't look up words because we are too confident. We may have seen a word many times, but we might not be able to write out a precise definition, pronounce it, or use it correctly in a sentence.

With this book, you can stay in your chair. We have scoured tens of thousands of pages in newspapers, magazines, and novels. Whenever we ran across a word that we weren't sure of, we considered it for the book. Because *Word Smart I* and *II* already contain many more commonly used words, it was easy to come up with words that were one step harder. We feel confident that these are challenging and useful words, even for those with strong vocabularies.

FUN AND GAMES

In addition, we found a good number of words that are rare, but fun to know. For example, we included the words "omphaloskepsis" (meditation by contemplating one's navel), and "groak" (one who hangs around waiting for a free meal). Maybe we can encourage you to bring some of these words back into circulation. ("My uncle is such a groak, arriving at six o'clock every night, napkin in tow.") Although only a small percentage of *Word Smart Genius Edition* includes these rare words, we hope that you find them enjoyable.

Be a Better Communicator

The great thing about learning words is that words help you think more clearly and exactly. By knowing the right word for any person, situation or problem, you can describe subtle distinctions. In writing this book, we have achieved a much more exact understanding of certain situations and can more succinctly explain ourselves. For example, the other day at a party, we saw this annoying guy Chad. He was preening in front of the mirror, worrying about his clothes, and ignoring us when we spoke. After working on this book for a while, one of us leaped up and said "Eureka! I know what Chad's problem is." We all sat with bated breath until she said, "Chad is a coxcomb." She was absolutely right.

Impress People

One sure sign of how educated you are is the number of words you know. On average, a person in the U.S. has a working vocabulary of 3,000 words, while a college graduate knows about 7,000. But with effort, it is possible to extend your working vocabulary to 20,000 words. (Before you get too impressed with your potential, remember that there are more than 750,000 words in the English language.) We feel that the 670 words described in this book can become impressive tools in your vocabulary arsenal.

There's More to These Words Than a Mere Definition

In researching these words, we found that many had fascinating stories behind them, and, whenever appropriate, we have included these etymologies. The English language is alive and constantly growing. Of the 750,000 words in English, more than eighty percent are originally from another language. In exploring the origins of words, you acquire a panoply of cultural and historical knowledge. You'll be astounded by the richness of the English language.

How This Book Is Organized

The first part of this book is a preliminary exam to test your knowledge of the words. It will give you an idea of how much studying you need to do to learn the vocabulary that follows. The best way to learn new words is to work slowly and consistently. With this in mind, we have placed a quiz to test your knowledge after every group of ten words. After the word lists, there is a final exam that tests your progress. This is an excellent means to make sure that you have retained your new vocabulary.

Speaking of Dictionaries . . .

In writing this book, we used four primary texts: the *Random House Unabridged Dictionary*, *Webster's Third New International Dictionary*, the *American Heritage Dictionary*, and the *Oxford English Dictionary*. The *OED* it includes an incredible amount of information on each word. The people who write the *OED* have embarked on the Sisyphean task of recording the uses of every word in the English language. Each entry starts with the word and its derivation, like other dictionaries, but it also includes, wherever possible, the first usage of the word, archaic or obsolete meanings, and sentences from different literary works.

There's More!

We have included a section on crossword puzzles, because there are certain words that, although rare in English, are common in crosswords. We think that if you learn the words, you will become a successful cruciverbalist.

We have also added a section on special words for animals. While you know that you should use the word "pride" to describe a group of lions, you may not know the correct word for a group of cats or a group of leopards. All of this information is included in a chart at the back of the book.

Enjoy

This is the best vocabulary book around. Spend some time learning these words and you will find that your thinking is clearer, and that you rarely see a word you don't know. Good luck, and bon verbiage.

Chapter 1

THE PRELIMINARY EXAMS

PRELIMINARY EXAM 1

Pronunciation

Pronounce each of the following words without looking at Column A or Column B. Then select the column that comes closer to your pronunciation.

		Column A	Column B
1.	scion	SKYE uhn	SYE uhn
2.	hegira	heh JYE ruh	heh JEE ruh
3.	aegis	AY ee juhs	EE juhs
4.	otiose	OH tee ohs	OH shee ohs
5.	farrago	fuh RAH goh	FAR uh goh
6.	patois	PA twah	PAY tohs
7.	paean	PAY ee uhn	PEE uhn
8.	igneous	IG nee uhs	ig NEY uhs
9.	bathos	BAH thahs	BAY thahs
10.	ecce homo	e kay HOH moh	e chay HOH moh
11.	couvade	KOO vayd	koo VAHD
12.	imbroglio	uhm BROHL yoh	im BROHG lee oh
13.	adjure	uh JUR	AHD juhr
14.	wreak	REHK	REEK
15.	fustian	FUHS tee uhn	FUHS chuhn
16.	fusillade	FYOO suh lahd	FYOO suh layd
17.	synecdoche	sih NEK duh kee	sih nek DOH chee
18.	abstemious	ab STEM ee uhs	abz TEE mee us
19.	wunderkind	WAWN duhr kuhn	VAWN duh kint
20.	rapprochement	RAH prohch ment	ra prohsh MAH

PRELIMINARY EXAM 2

Definitions

For each question below, match the word on the left with its definition on the right.

1. portmanteau
2. sedulous
3. caduceus
4. craquelure
5. simulacrum
6. dolor
7. chthonic
8. viridescent
9. ziggurat

a. cracks on oil paintings
b. green
c. stepped pyramid
d. painstaking
e. related to netherworld
f. suitcase
g. Hermes staff
h. sorrow
i. image

PRELIMINARY EXAM 3

Definitions

For each question below, match the word on the left with its definition on the right.

1. chirr
2. Pablum
3. umbrage
4. cuckold
5. panache
6. opus
7. garrote
8. genuflect
9. ecumenical

a. baby gruel
b. universal
c. harsh sound
d. strangle
e. creative work
f. curtsy
g. cheated on man
h. displeasure
i. verve

PRELIMINARY EXAM 4

Definitions
For each question below, match the word on the left with its definition on the right.

1. plenary	a. enormous creature
2. groak	b. weeping
3. lachrymose	c. full
4. tenebrous	d. one who watches eaters to get food
5. deliquesce	e. postulate
6. posit	f. dark
7. propinquity	g. melt away
8. behemoth	h. proximity
9. arrogate	i. to appropriate

PRELIMINARY EXAM 5

Definitions
For each question below, match the word on the left with its definition on the right.

1. conation	a. coup
2. verbiage	b. later
3. putsch	c. confuse
4. integument	d. medley
5. anon	e. wordiness
6. feckless	f. envelope
7. discombobulate	g. lively person
8. salmagundi	h. will
9. fulsome	i. offensively excessive

Chapter 2

THE WORDS

ABECEDARIAN *n.* (ay bee see DAR ee uhn) a person who teaches or studies the alphabet; a person who is learning the alphabet for the first time *adj.* relating to the alphabet; alphabetical; elementary or basic

The older child, entering the third grade, was proud to help her younger brother, an *abecedarian*.

The first few months of kindergarten were spent almost entirely on *abecedarian* tasks.

Many of the Bible's psalms are *abecedarian*, that is, they are organized in alphabetical order.

ABLATE *v.* (uh BLAYT) to remove through erosion or evaporation; to become reduced by erosion or evaporation

The earth's atmosphere is efficient at protecting us from falling meteorites because it is dense enough to *ablate* and break up most falling matter before it hits the surface.

Even the hardest rock will *ablate* given enough exposure to the continual turbulence of ocean waves.

ABLUTION *n.* (uh BLOO shun) or (a BLOO shun) the act of cleansing one's body (esp. as part of a religious rite); the liquid used in such an act

After completing many of the prescribed rituals, the rajah begged leave to perform his *ablutions*.

The Hindu religion is full of *ablutionary* rites, and its adherents, therefore, manage to stay very clean.

ABREACTION *n.* (AB ree ak shun) or (ab ree AK shun) the release of pent-up emotions through verbalizing a previous event that caused a conflict or catharsis (psychology)

Abreaction is a word used in psychology to describe the resulting release of emotions engendered through acting out a previous event. A person abreacts the emotions associated with an event by discussing it with her therapist, and this action helps alleviate tensions caused by the event. The word is very similar to one of the meanings of catharsis, although catharsis can also mean the release of emotions through the arts.

The early attempts to get him to *abreact* his hostility over his younger brother's theft of a bowl of soup failed, and as a result, the two haven't spoken in years.

ABSINTHE n. (AB sinth) or (AB suhnth) a perennial herb called Wormwood (*Artemisia absinthium*) found in Europe; a green liquor, with a high percentage of alcohol, made from absinthe (now illegal in many countries) (also absinth)

People who drank lots of absinthe (sufferers of absinthism) became the subject for many paintings during the post-impressionist period of the late 19th century. Artists like Degas were fascinated by the legions of down-and-out absinthe addicts who congregated night after night in bars throughout Europe. Ernest Hemingway was a big fan of the drink. Wormwood was thought to have first grown in the track left by the serpent after he was barred from Eden.

After Napoleon came into our boîte and conscripted my three sons to fight in the war, I took several glasses of *absinthe* to steady my nerves.

ABSQUATULATE v. (abz KWACH uh layt) or (ab SKACH uh layt) to decamp

This Americanism, a combination of the root "abs" (off, away from), "squat" (to sit in slang), and "ulate" (like in speculate of gratulate), is a humorous way of saying to break camp, to unsquat (so to speak). It is slang, but an effective way of expressing a deliberate exit.

Disturbed by our shouting, the enormous buffalo sleepily raised its head and began to *absquatulate* into the wilderness.

ABSTEMIOUS adj. (abz TEE mee us) eating or drinking little; refraining from enjoyment in pleasures of any kind; marked by abstinence

Abstemious is derived from the Latin "abs" (away from) and "te-me-tum" (intoxicating liquor), but even when used in Latin the word meant temperance in general. Although the roots of the words abstemious and abstain are different, the similarity in sound between the two words has helped extend the meaning of abstemious.

The Dahli Lama believes in an *abstemious* way of life. His *abstemiousness* has been noted by many, who are surprised at how little he consumes in a day.

Although not a teetotaler, Maurice was remarkably *abstemious* and has yet to experience a hangover.

ACIDULOUS adj. (uh SIJ uh lus) somewhat sour, having a degree of acidity; sour-tempered

One of the qualities of gold is that it is resistant to *acidulous* agents.
Before his morning coffee, he is somewhat gloomy and *acidulous*.

ADJURE v. (uh JUR) to command earnestly

Even though the judge *adjured* the young witness to speak the truth, the jury did not believe him and the accused went free.

The professor *adjured* all of her students to at least make an effort to use correct grammar.

ADUMBRATE *v.* (AD uhm brayt) to give an indistinct outline of; to foreshadow; to disclose only a part of something

Part of the new employee's worries about the job stemmed from the fact that his duties were not spelled out in detail, but rather *adumbrated*.

The method by which the Nazis used false showers to kill Jews after 1942 was *adumbrated* by pre-war Nazi techniques for euthanasia of the mentally ill.

QUICK QUIZ #1

Match each word in the first column with its definition in the second column. Check your answers in the back.

1. abecedarian	a. wear away
2. ablate	b. beg
3. ablution	c. foreshadow
4. abreaction	d. abstinent
5. absinthe	e. to decamp
6. absquatulate	f. sour
7. abstemious	g. washing one's body
8. acidulous	h. green liquor
9. adjure	i. catharsis
10. adumbrate	j. alphabetical

AEGIS *n.* (EE juhs) protection; sponsorship (also egis)

Aegis originally referred to the breastplate of Zeus that featured the head of Medusa. Since Medusa's visage would turn a potential attacker to stone, the shield protected its bearer. The word is now used to mean sponsorship or protection, as in "under the aegis of."

Under the *aegis* of Duke Ellington, the individual musicians were able to develop a collective style that was better than the sum of its parts.

AFFECTIVE *adj.* (A fek tiv) or (a FEK tiv) or (uh FEK tiv) emotional; expressing emotion

This word is used in psychology to express the emotional aspects of personality. It is usually contrasted with cognitive and conative.

His education enlarged the cognitive sphere of his ability, because teachers did not deem it their responsibility to instruct in the *affective*.

AGATHISM *n.* (A guh thiz uhm) the belief that all things ultimately lead to good.

Agathism is different from optimism in that an optimist believes that all is now for the best, while an agathist believes that all will turn out okay in the end. For most people we usually consider optimists, agathist is a more erudite choice.

The *agathist* corrected his student. "I am not an optimist," he said, "I believe that there are many problems in the world; I am convinced that they will get better."

AGNATE *adj.* (AG nayt) or (AYG nayt) from the father's side of a family *n.* an actual relative from the father's side.

Although agnate is not often used today, it can be useful in replacing the cumbersome "my grandmother on my father's side" with the much more elegant "agnate grandmother." The word for a relative on one's mother's side is "enate."

My *agnate* grandmother met my enate grandmother for lunch and realized that I had given them identical birthday gifts.

AGOG *adv., adj.* (uh GOG) very excited, impatiently eager

While waiting for the train to take him home, the soldier was all *agog* about his homecoming.

Houdini would spend a few minutes talking up his act, and when the audience was *agog*, he would allow himself to be held upside down in handcuffs in a locked milk jug.

AILUROPHILE *n.* (eye LUH ruh fyel) or (Ay LUR ruh fyel) a cat lover

Ailur is from the Greek for cat. An ailurophile loves cats; an "ailurophobe" (eye LUH ruh fohb) is afraid of cats.

A confessed *ailurophile*, Dahlia took care of seventeen cats in her home. Unfortunately for Dahlia, her fiancé was an ailurophobe.

AKIMBO *adv., adj.* (uh KIM boh) having one's hands on one's hips; being in a bent or bowed position

Although akimbo is most often used to describe one's arms in a bent position with hands on hips, it has recently been used to describe legs as well. A person whose limbs are akimbo holds them in an awkward position. The word also has a figurative sense; for example, one might speak of an akimbo melodic line.

Obviously fatigued from her valiant attempts at winning the game single-handedly, the basketball star stood dejected, arms *akimbo*, waiting for the final buzzer to sound.

ALEATORY *adj.* (AY lee a toh ree) based on chance or uncertain prospect

The word derives from a French word for a dice thrower.

Using such an *aleatory* process to choose a home seems to risk trouble in the future.

The *aleatory* contract between the government and the mining concern would work out well for the company if the land contained gold.

AMANUENSIS *n.* (uh man yuh WEN suhs) someone who takes dictation or copies manuscripts

Despite his prodigious talent as an artist, Yusef Kernal spend most of his time working as an *amanuensis*, jotting down the mundane musings of an illiterate bank president.

AMARANTH *n.* (A muh ranth) an imaginary flower that does not fade; a flower of the genus Amaranthus; a deep purple with a reddish tinge

    The painting had succeeded so well in capturing the rose that the image had become an immortal *amaranth*.

Quick Quiz #2

Match each word in the first column with its definition in the second column. Check your answers in the back.

1. aegis	a. sponsorship
2. affective	b. optimism
3. agathism	c. eager
4. agnate	d. cat lover
5. agog	e. father's
6. ailurophile	f. flower that lasts forever
7. akimbo	g. random
8. aleatory	h. stenographer
9. amanuensis	i. bent
10. amaranth	j. emotional

AMICUS CURIAE *n.* (uh MEE kuh scyuh ree eye) or (uh mee kuh SCYUH ree eye) a non-involved participant in a court case

    This word means literally in Latin "friend of the court."
    The National Committee for Tax Awareness filed an *amicus curiae* brief in the Felmsey tax evasion case.

ANOMIE *n.* (A nuh mee) the resultant instability caused by an erosion of values; lack of purpose caused by erosion of values; unsocial behavior caused by a person's disorganization (also anomia and anomy)

    Anomie is a good word to use if you need to describe the way in which our modern world is "going to pot."
    "As we approach the *fin de siècle*," house leader Gwenn Critigh remarked "we exist in a condition of *anomie*; only through the destruction of government as we know it can we bring about a return to good ol' American values."
    Children raised in a condition of *anomie* are much less likely to achieve success later in life.

ANON *adv.* (uh NAHN) later; soon

    Anon is sometimes used in the idioms "now and anon" and "ever and anon" both of which mean from time to time.
    We live now, we shall die *anon*.
    Her world crashing around her and her family ruined, ever and *anon* a tear appeared in her eye.

ANTEDILUVIAN *adj.* (AN tee duh loo vee uhn) or (an tee duh LOO vee uhn) extremely old (with a negative connotation)

Antediluvian mean literally "before the biblical flood" and can be used that way.

According to the Bible, people in *antediluvian* times certainly lived a lot longer than we do today.

After having heard tales of his venerable family home for months, his fiancée was surprised to see a sorry *antediluvian* shack which swayed unsteadily in the ocean breeze.

A related word is antebellum, which means literally "before the war," but is used most often when referring to the American Civil War.

Conditions in the *antebellum* south were certainly a lot better than those after the war.

APHASIA *n.* (uh FAY zhuh) or (uh FAY zhee uh) an inability to understand or articulate spoken or written language caused by brain injury or disease

The accident wasn't severe, but the doctors administered the anesthesia incorrectly, causing complete sensory *aphasia*; the patient could not comprehend anything.

APODICTIC *adj.* (A puh dik tik) or (a puh DIK tik) unequivocally true

An apodictic statement is one that is clearly true and easily proved. An argumentative person might make his case by stating his premises apodictically.

The listener stood with mouth agape, uncertain how to respond to such a heinous statement made with such *apodictic* certainty.

APOGEE *n.* (AP uh jee) the point of a moon or an artificial satellite when it is as far away as possible from the center of its orbit; the apex or highest point

The moon will reach its *apogee* on the 15th of this month. As the moon moves about the earth approximately once a month, it reaches its *apogee* about once a month.

U.S. power in international affairs was at a new high immediately after WWII, but it had by no means reached its *apogee*.

APOSIOPESIS *n.* (a puh sye uh PEE suhs) an abrupt breaking off of an idea or thought in the middle of a sentence that suggests the speaker did not want to or was unable to continue; a rhetorical artifice

The speech was contrived so exactly that the audience was convinced that the President's *aposiopesis* was unplanned, believing him to be too upset to continue rambling on about a truly noble person corrupted by the vagaries of the welfare state.

ARGOT *n.* (AHR guht) a dialect of a particular group. Thieves' argot is a cant (KANT).

The speaker's lowly origins became known as soon as she opened her mouth and spoke her uncouth *argot*.

In the quaint *argot* of the period, a smirking gamine might be described as "smiling like a Cheshire cat."

ARRIVISTE *n.* (a ree VEEST) or (A ree veest) a person who has achieved a high position through unscrupulous means; one who seeks such a position, a social climber

An unashamed *arriviste*, John felt no remorse after spreading nasty and unsubstantiated rumors about the private life of his superiors.

Quick Quiz #3

Match each word in the first column with its definition in the second column. Check your answers in the back.

1. amicus curiae	a. social instability
2. anomie	b. far point
3. anon	c. dialect
4. antediluvian	d. later
5. aphasia	e. abrupt halt in speech
6. apodictic	f. incontrovertible
7. apogee	g. outside adviser in a court case
8. aposiopesis	h. inability to express ideas
9. argot	i. vulgar social climber
10. arriviste	j. ancient

ARROGATE *v.* (AR ruh gayt) to appropriate without right, to make undue claim to, assume; to appropriate for another in an unwarranted manner

This word, appropriately enough, comes from the same Latin root "arrogant." An arrogant person, in a sense, appropriates more consideration or talent than he is worth. In the same way, to arrogate is to appropriate without right.

The speaker of the house had *arrogated* the President's responsibility to set the policy agenda for the country.

His henchmen attempted to *arrogate* the power of the parliament for the newly crowned King of England.

ASSIGNATION *n.* (a sig NAY shun) assignment; something assigned; a tryst, a date between two lovers

Assignation can also mean something assigned (e.g. the property rights were transmissible by simple assignation).

Having to work late made it impossible for the lecherous detective to keep his *assignation*.

ATAVISM *n.* (AD uh viz uhm) or (AT uh viz uhm) the reappearance or return of a previous trait after a period in which the trait had not appeared; an individual or a part that exhibits atavism

With parents, grandparents and great-grandparents all having green or brown eyes, the infant's blue eyes were some mysterious *atavism* of a distant ancestor.

ATRABILIOUS *adj.* (A truh bil yuhs) or (a truh BIL yuhs) surly, peevish; inclined to melancholy

Such a profession of love, so sweetly and gently expressed, was bound to cheer even the most *atrabilious* curmudgeon.

AUTO-DA-FÉ *n.* (au toh duh FAY) burning a heretic at the stake; public announcements of the sentence given a heretic during the inquisition; the carrying out of such sentence.

The plural of auto-da-fé is autos-da-fé.

After the inquisition and its awful *autos-da-fé*, today's lethal injections seem humane by comparison.

AVATAR *n.* (AV uh tahr) an archetype; a temporary incarnation of a continuing entity; the embodiment of a Hindu deity, esp. Vishnu

With his peripatetic wanderings and life lived in the wayward rhythms of bebop, Jack Kerouac was an *avatar* of the beat generation.

Krishna is considered by Hindi worshipers to be the *avatar* of Vishnu.

AVER *v.* (uh VUHR) declare, assert; in law, to assert formally or to prove

While Galileo Galilei *averred* that the Earth moved around the sun, his accusers denied that any such possibility existed.

The attorney *averred* the nefarious Col. Mustard's guilt by matching the fingerprints from the candlestick.

BABBITT *n.* (BA buht) a member of the middle class who is so fond of its ideals as to be narrow minded and conceited

Babbitt is derived from the name of a hero in a 1922 Sinclair Lewis novel, a narrow minded businessman who conformed to the expectations of his cohort.

After spending years in a land where all were *Babbitts*, Yuseff was happy to find a group of intellectuals who loved poetry and the arts.

BADINAGE *n.* (bad uhn AHZH) repartee, jovial banter

While she was known for discussing only the deepest truths, her husband kept the parties light by engaging in playful *badinage*.

BAGATELLE *n.* (bag uh TEL) or (BAG uh tell) something of insignificance, a trifle; a short piece of music

The vast amount of money that billionaire Tom Prose spent in the 1992 election was *bagatelle* compared to the billion-dollar tax cut given to him by the government in the seventies.

Although Beethoven is known for the puissance of his symphonic works, he also wrote many cheery *bagatelles*.

QUICK QUIZ #4

Match each word in the first column with its definition in the second column. Check your answers in the back.

1. arrogate	a. banter
2. assignation	b. peevish
3. atavism	c. reoccurence of a trait
4. atrabilious	d. archetype
5. auto-da-fé	e. tryst
6. avatar	f. triffle
7. aver	g. burning at the stake
8. Babbitt	h. to appropriate
9. badinage	i. declare
10. bagatelle	j. bougeoise

BAILIWICK *n.* (BAY lee wik) or (BAY luh wik) one's particular area of expertise

Although he felt a dilettante's pleasure in discussing particle physics, he knew not to say much around his aunt (an expert in the field) lest he intrude upon her *bailiwick*.

BALDERDASH *n.* (BAWL duhr dash) nonsense, trash

For all his pedantic traits, his friends were often surprised at the phalanx of *balderdash* that lined his bookshelves.

BANAUSIC *adj.* (buh NAW sik) routine or mechanical, boring

After being overwhelmed by the brilliance of his last play, Mary was disappointed in having to sit through such *banausic* tripe.

BARRATOR *n.* (BAR ruhd uhr) one that is constantly filing suits, esp. false and malicious suits (also barrater)

Some of the seediest law firms in the city survive by having a tassel of lawyers whose sole job is to sue people maliciously. These *barrators* file suits in the hope that the accused party will settle out of court to avoid the hassle of a court case.

BASTINADO *n.* (bas tuh NAY doh) a beating; a form of punishment in which a person is hit on the soles of his feet with a stick

He tried to explain to his father that *bastinado* was unjust punishment for stealing a cookie.

BATHOS *n.* (BAY thahs) a sudden transition from the illustrious to the commonplace; insincere or overdone pathos; triteness, banality

The address at commencement produced gales of laughter when the distinguished senator's speech degenerated to *bathos*: "As graduates you have the responsibility to continue in your education, to help your communities, and to pay all outstanding parking tickets."

His writing degenerated after the death of his mother from clear unemotional prose to language that was sentimental to the brink of *bathos*.

BAVARDAGE *n.* (ba vuhr DAHZH) chatter, idle talk

Sick of the students' *bavardage*, the elementary school teacher slammed a yardstick onto her desk and shocked the students into silence.

BEAMISH *adj.* (BEEM ish) smiling or glowing

After the war ended, Americans everywhere were *beamish*, ecstatic that they would soon be entering a long period of peace and prosperity.

BEDIZEN *v.* (beh DYE zuhn) or (beh DI zuhn) to dress in a gaudy fashion

The lottery winner arrived at the congratulatory party *bedizened* in the most expensive purple suit that he could find.

BEGUINE *n.* (be GEEN) or (bay GEEN) a kind of popular dance, associated with Martinique; *adj.* syncopated beat

This word comes from the French word "béguin" (bay GAN), for flirtation, and originally described a dance step from Martinique. It became more well-known in the U.S. after Cole Porter named a popular song "Begin the Beguine."

The band started playing and the dancers' legs began to shimmy to the *beguine* rhythms of the great Duke Ellington.

Samantha spent her nights in Martinique dancing the *beguine* with her lover, Gus.

QUICK QUIZ #5

1. bailiwick	a. nonsense
2. balderdash	b. syncopated
3. banausic	c. cudgeling
4. barrator	d. ambulance chaser
5. bastinado	e. chatter
6. bathos	f. dress gaudilly
7. bavardage	g. anticlimax
8. beamish	h. smiling
9. bedizen	i. expertise
10. beguine	j. mechanical

BEHEMOTH *n.* (buh HEE muhth) or (bee HEE muhth) something that is enormous

A behemoth is originally described in the Old Testament as a large animal.

"Behold now *behemoth*, which I made with thee; he eateth grass as an ox. Lo now, his strength is in his loins, and his force is in the navel of his belly."

—From the Book of Job, the Bible

BELDAM *n*. (BEL duhm) or (BEL dam) an ugly old woman; a raging woman (also beldame)

Entering the room, our hero was descended upon by a cadre of fat *beldams* screaming words of advice as to how to avoid capture.

BESMIRCH *v*. (buh SMUHRCH) or (bee SMUHRCH) to stain or sully, esp. a reputation

The muddy footprints of the workmen *besmirched* the linoleum tile of the kitchen.

The rumors of infidelity *besmirched* the politician's reputation.

BÊTE NOIRE *n*. (bet nuh WAHR) or (bet NWAHR) something that is detested

This word is derived literally from the French meaning "Black Beast," and it refers to something that is particularly disliked.

Taxes have long been the *bêtes noires* of big business.

After the defeat of Sadaam Hussein, the American government was on the lookout for a new *bete noire*.

BIBELOT *n*. (BEE buh low) or (BEE blow) a bauble, a small decorative object; a finely crafted miniature book

Upon entering the dilapidated home of her fiancé's family, Sarita was astonished at the sheer number of *bibelots* strewn about.

BIBULOUS *adj*. (BIB yuh luhs) given to or marked by drinking alcohol; very absorbent

Larry felt that it was about time to celebrate years of abstemious behavior with a *bibulous* evening.

Because of their *bibulous* quality, the new paper towels can effectively absorb liquid that is 300 times their own weight.

BILGE *n*. (BILJ) a nautical term meaning the rounded part of a ship's hull; the water that collects within the lowest part of the ship's hull. In slang it means stupid talk; nonsense.

This word is most likely a corrupted form of the word "bulge." Although you might not have much use for the literal meaning of this nautical term (unless you are in a leaky boat on the Potomac bailing out the bilge) its figurative sense is evocative of the effluvia that you might expect to collect in the bottom of a boat.

"The *bilge* constantly flowing out that silly boy's mouth just makes me sick!" Sue Beth said, rolling her eyes.

BIRKIE *adj*. (BIR ki) or (BUHR ki) lively; spirited; *n*. a man who is lively or spirited

Even though this word is used primarily in Scotland, it seems such an onomatopoetically perfect way to describe a lively or spirited man that we are including it in this book. A birkie is usually meant as a compliment to describe a crusty self assertive man, but it can also be a bit deprecatory.

After working her way through the mostly passive interviewees, Ms. Samuals was pleased to meet such a *birkie* fellow.

BISSEXTILE DAY *n.* (bye SEKS tuhl) the 29th of February on a leap year

Unlucky enough to be born on *bissextile day*, Maureen's sweet-sixteen party was celebrated on her fourth birthday.

BODKIN *n.* (BAHD kuhn) a small, but sharply pointed tool for making holes in leather or fabric; a long hairpin

In England, bodkin is used figuratively to describe a person squished tightly between two others.

While the first part of the trip was enjoyable, the second half was unpleasant because she had to sit *bodkin* between two corpulent and sweaty men.

QUICK QUIZ #6

Match each word in the first column with its definition in the second column. Check your answers in the back.

1. behemoth	a. hag
2. beldam	b. trinket
3. besmirch	c. nonsense
4. bête noire	d. soil
5. bibelot	e. one to be avoided
6. bibulous	f. drunken
7. bilge	g. lively man
8. birkie	h. hole maker
9. bissextile day	i. Feb-29
10. bodkin	j. enormous

BOILERPLATE *n.* (BOYL uhr playt) steel plate used for making the outside of boilers; syndicated material for journalism that used to come in plate form; formulaic or inconsequential language

Originally many syndicated features in newspapers arrived as one steel plate which could be easily replicated in a newspaper. These features were often written in a formulaic style that would appeal to the masses, and by extension, bad formulaic writing came to be known as boilerplate.

The creative abilities clearly shown in her first novel were lacking in her second, which was little more than *boilerplate*.

BOÎTE *n.* (bwaht) a small restaurant, a joint

This word comes from a French word meaning literally "night box."

After three months of working in Paris, the pair finally had time to experience the night life. They ate out at a nice restaurant and then skipped happily to a *boîte* where they danced and drank till the wee hours of the morning.

BOMBILATION *n.* (bahm buh LAY shun) buzzing, humming sound. This is from the Latin word "bombit" (to buzz).

The *bombilation* of the honeybees swarming the budding trees is a sure sign of spring.

BONHOMIE *n.* (BAHN uh mee) a genial disposition (sometimes bonhommie)

One who has bonhomie is good natured and easy to get along with. The word can also describe a genial atmosphere.

The Christmas *bonhomie* of the past has given way to a less congenial spirit, one where shoppers scream at clerks, and families bicker about everything including the turkey.

BORBORYGMUS *n.* (bawr buh RIG muhs) a noise made by one's stomach when gas moves through the intestine

It is perhaps unfortunate that the word that describes such a common occurrence is so uncommon, but borborygmus is the exact term to describe that embarrassing rumbling that resonates from our insides.

The room became silent except for the *borborygmi* of a thousand empty stomachs.

BOWDLERIZE *v.* (BOWD luh ryez) to censor prudishly

The word comes from Dr. T. Bowdler who published an edition of Shakespeare in which anything that "cannot with propriety be read aloud in a family" was omitted. Bowdler wanted to make the plays fit for "the perusal of our virtuous females."

Even though the diaries stretched the limit of what's acceptable, the editor resisted the urge to *bowdlerize;* the unexpurgated edition succeeded in creating quite a scandal.

BOWER *n.* (BAUHR) a cottage or abode; a shelter in a garden made of tree limbs (also bowery)

After the grand party in the mansion of F. Scott Fitzgerald, we all drove over to their secret *bower*, tucked away behind a hillock in a beautiful forest glen.

BRAY *v.* (BRAY) to crush into powder

The word was used in the King James Version of the Bible: "Though thou shuldest *bray* a foole with a pestell in a morter like otemeell, yet wil not his foolishnesse go from him." (Proverbs xxvii. 22) and the expression is still used to refer to educating a fool.

To make the curry powder, Kemala first *brayed* the spices in a mortar and then sautéed the spices in a cast iron pan.

BROOK *v.* (bruhk) to tolerate or endure

The chairman had had enough of the petty bickering about the new proposal and insisted that he would *brook* no further discussion.

BRUIT *n.* (BROOT) to pass news of; repeat

    Rumors about his relationship with Little Suzy were *bruited* about the classroom.

QUICK QUIZ #7

Match each word in the first column with its definition in the second column. Check your answers in the back.

1. boilerplate	a. cottage
2. boîte	b. formulaic language
3. bombilation	c. humming sound
4. bonhomie	d. crush
5. borborygmus	e. geniality
6. bowdlerize	f. repeat
7. bower	g. censor
8. bray	h. stomach rumble
9. brook	i. nightclub
10. bruit	j. tolerate

BUMPTIOUS *adj.* (BUHM shuhs) pushy; conceited; loudly assertive

    A bumptious person is one who would bump you out of the way.

    Despite being somewhat reserved at home, Newt was *bumptious* at work, imperiously commanding his subordinates to either do his bidding or find another job.

    The *bumptious* sergeant stood so close to me that his feet were touching mine and his putrid breath was tickling my nose. "Attention" he bellowed, and I collapsed in a heap!

BUNKUM *n.* (BUHN kuhm) claptrap; empty or insincere chatter

    This word comes from a widely publicized incident during a debate about the Missouri Compromise in which Felix Walker, a Congressman from Buncombe, North Carolina wanted to speak even though the rest of the house wanted to vote. The congressman declared that he had to "make a speech for Buncombe," and Buncombe became synonymous with empty chatter.

    The speech was pure *bunkum* and everyone knew it except the speaker, who was soon forcibly removed from the stage.

BURKE *v.* (BUHRK) to suppress quietly or stifle; to disregard; to kill someone through suffocation

    William Burke, a criminal who was executed in England in 1829, was accused of suffocating people and selling their bodies for dissection. The word burke has come to mean to extinguish something quietly (and completely).

His expose into the private lives of Madonna's retinue was *burked* by the publishing company (which was a subsidiary of her record company).

Rather than confront the problems with his employer, Samuel *burked* the issue and continued to work diligently.

CACHET *n.* (ka SHAY) or (KA shay) a mark or quality of distinction or authenticity; prestige; an indication of approval

This word originally referred to a seal, especially one used to seal a letter from a king which contained news of an execution or prison sentence. Now used figuratively more than literally, a cachet indicates a mark or recognition of distinction or approval.

Although he had to pay more money each month to buy the apartment, owning a place gave him a *cachet* of respectability that pleased him.

CACHINNATE *v.* (KA kuh nayt) to laugh really hard; to guffaw

To cachinnate is to laugh uncontrollably in an especially immoderate way.

I was suddenly aware of the fact that everyone around me was *cachinnating* even though there had been no apparent joke.

CADUCEUS *n.* (kuh DOO see uhs) Hermes' staff which had two serpents entwined around it; the symbol used to represent the medical profession.

This is one of those words that, unless you study the classics, will only be useful because it allows you to use the correct word to describe something.

That crazy symbol by the door to the hospital is a *caduceus.*

CADUCITY *n.* (kuh DOO suhd EE) the infirmities of old age; transitoriness

After living a vigorous life, the octogenarian was forced to confront his *caducity* after the symptoms of Alzheimer's became more noticeable.

CALLIPYGIAN *adj.* (kal uh PIJ ee uhn) or (KAL uh pij ee uhn) having shapely buttocks

This word derives from the Greek "Kallos" (beauty as used in calligraphy) and "Pyge" (buttocks) In a Naples museum there is a famous statue of Aphrodite named Callipygius, which, as you might imagine, looks better from the rear.

It's a lucky day at the beach when the surf is high and *callipygian* bathers are everywhere.

CAMORRA *n.* (kuh MAWR ruh) a secret Neapolitan society organized in the 1820s similar to the Mafia; any secret group

Well organized and clandestine, the *camorra* has been able to reap enormous profits.

CANARD *n.* (kuh NAHRD) a false, intentionally misleading story

Lexicographers have two theories as to the derivation of this word. One is that it derives from the old French expression "vendre un canard à moitié" meaning (to half-sell a duck) or make a fool of someone. The other theory is that it derives from an exaggerated tale about the voracity of a particular duck that was widely repeated in newspapers for a time. In either case, the French word for "duck" became the English word for a intentionally misleading story.

Recently a crazy little *canard* has been circulating in the White House about the licentious habits of the first cat.

Quick Quiz #8

Match each word in the first column with its definition in the second column. Check your answers in the back.

1. bumptious		a. pushy
2. bunkum		b. mafia
3. burke		c. suffocate
4. cachet		d. guffaw
5. cachinnate		e. nice butt
6. caduceus		f. senility
7. caducity		g. Hermes staff
8. callipygian		h. tall tale
9. camorra		i. mark of distinction
10. canard		j. claptrap

CANOODLE *v.* (kuh NOOD uhl) to caress or make love; to persuade through caressing

As soon as they entered the home of her fiancé's parents, she knew there was to be trouble. His mother, seeing his arm around her, said "As long as I'm a-here watchin', there ain't gonna be no *canoodling* in my house."

CAPTIOUS *adj.* (KAP shus) having a tendency to uncover and mention trivial faults; intended to confuse

The C.E.O. was *captious*, making little difficulties for her employees at every turn. A staple on the wrong side of the paper was enough to send her into paroxysms of ire.

CARYATID *n.* (kar ee AD uhd) or (KAR ee uh tid) a column used for support that is shaped like a draped female figure

The two enormous *caryatids* seemed to strain holding up the enormous pediment with the Iliadic frieze carved onto its marble surface.

CASSANDRA *n.* (kuh SAN druh) a person whose predictions or prophecies go unheeded

Based on the Greek myth of Cassandra who was given the power of prophecy but was doomed by Apollo to have her prophesies unheeded.

Cassandra's warnings that world-wide temperatures were rising went unheeded and subsequently coastal cities were flooded with sea water.

CATACHRESIS *n.* (ka ta KREE suhs) the improper use of a word or phrase, esp. when for effect

The speaker was pleased when his *catachresis* brought forth gales of laughter. "This city," he had said, "is as clean as a baby's bottom."

The wordmongers of the world had noticed a general *catachresis* of "blatant" when "flagrant" was called for.

CELERITY *n.* (suh LER uhd ee) or (suh LER uh tee) haste, swiftness of movement or action, especially the movements of living beings

The *celerity* of the squirrel's movement caught Ella unaware, dashing the cat's hopes for an easy meal.

CENOBITE *n.* (SEN uh byet) a person who belongs to a convent (also coenobite)

A cenobite is different from, say, a hermit, in that a cenobite lives in a community.

After the example of Saint Bernard, some monks went to live on their own in the forest to discover true poverty and to get closer to god, while others lived as *cenobites*.

CHARNEL *adj.* (SHAHR nuhl) ghastly, suggesting death; a charnel house is a tomb; *n.* a tomb

After the body was placed in the *charnel* house, the last rites were read, and the silence of the dead reigned over the mortuary.

The *charnel* smell of the dead man's bones was enough to send the seasoned policeman into the arms of Jack Daniels.

CHARY *adj.* (CHA ree) wary, extremely cautious; sparing

It would have been crazy for even the most reckless driver to continue with the storm so close at hand, but for one as *chary* as Pat, a trip was unthinkable.

The patient knew she needed an operation, but was *chary* of the risks involved.

CHARYBDIS *n.* (kuh RIB duhs) a destructive hazard

Referred to in Homer's *Odyssey*, Charybdis is a dangerous whirlpool on the coast of Sicily. The whirlpool is directly across from the rock Scylla (SIL luh), and the phrase between Charybdis and Scylla has the same meaning as between a rock and a hard place.

For thirty years the former Yugoslavia was able to avoid the Scylla of Russian domination only to run into the *Charybdis* of extreme nationalism.

Miraculously, he was able to wind his way between the Scylla of the enormous semi and the *Charybdis* of oncoming traffic.

Quick Quiz #9

Match each word in the first column with its definition in the second column. Check your answers in the back.

1.	canoodle	a.	member of a convent
2.	captious	b.	unheeded prophet
3.	caryatid	c.	misuse of word
4.	Cassandra	d.	column
5.	catachresis	e.	caress
6.	celerity	f.	hazard
7.	cenobite	g.	tomb
8.	charnel	h.	hypercritical
9.	chary	i.	swiftness
10.	Charybdis	j.	cautious

CHATTEL n. (CHAD uhl) or (CHAT uhl) an object of portable personal property; a slave

The word chattel comes from the same English roots as cattle and represents movable personal property. Abolitionists applied the word to slaves to emphasize the dehumanizing aspects of slavery.

The bargain-hunters converged on the estate sale swiftly buying up any *chattel* that was available.

In ante-bellum South, slaves and other *chattel* could be willed to the next generation.

CHIAROSCURO n. (kyah ruh SKYOOHR oh) using light and shade for representation in painting or drawing; the arrangements of such elements in a work of art

Chiaroscuro, sometimes called claire-obscure (klar uhbz KYOOR), is a painting technique used often in the history of representative art. Da Vinci, for instance, whose paintings have dramatic shadows contrasting his figures, would be described as a master of chiaroscuro. Da Vinci is also known as a master of the technique of sfumato (sfoo MAH toh) in which the artist creates a form through a gradual change from light to dark. A close examination of the Mona Lisa will show that it is unclear exactly where her face ends and her hair begins. The lines surrounding an object are obscured, and a delicate atmospheric effect is created.

CHIRR n. (CHUHR) a harsh sound similar to that made by crickets

The word chirr is a relatively new word in the English language that seems to have derived in the seventeenth century from words like chirp, chirk, chirl, or chirm. All of these words have similar meanings, but the differences among them are suggested by their sound. A chirr is like a chirp or a chirk except that it continues for a longer period of time. A chirl starts like a chirp but descends into a warbling tone, and a chirm suggests a confused din, like that of many insects making noise at once.

It was the night before Christmas and all around the house, not a cricket was *chirring*, nor could be heard the scrip scrap scrape of a common louse.

CHTHONIC *adj.* (THAN ik) of or relating to the underworld (also chthonian)

This word comes from the Greek word Chthon, meaning Earth, and refers to both the Greek gods and other beings that live in the underworld. In philosophy and aesthetics, "chthonic" is often contrasted with "Olympian" which refers to Mount Olympus where the gods reside. Something chthonic is dark and turbulent, while something Olympian is transcendent or lofty.

Achilles' mother dipped him in the *chthonic* river Styx to protect him against the swords of his enemies.

CINCTURE *n.* (SINK chuhr) enclosure, act of encircling; belt, girdle; *v.* to enclose, to encircle

The home of the mobster was surrounded by a moat filled with piranha, a 20-foot high wall, and a *cincture* of mines.

His robe, *cinctured* with a braided rope, was threadbare, his shoes non-existent, but he still walked with a regal bearing.

CIRCADIAN *adj.* (suhr KAY dee uhn) relating to a 24-hour period

The jet-lag he was feeling was obviously caused by a discombobulation of his *circadian* rhythms.

CLAMANT *adj.* (KLAY muhnt) or (kla muhnt) loud; demanding attention

There is nothing as loud as a deliriously *clamant* crowd in Madison Square Garden during the NBA basketball finals.

Though there seemed no evidence for his distress, Mark was in *clamant* need of calming.

CLAQUE *n.* (KLAK) a group of people paid to applaud during a performance; a group of obsequious admirers

The tepid and banal performance of *Rigoletto* should have brought jeers and catcalls, but instead, brought clamant applause from an obviously well-paid *claque*.

One of the unfortunate appendages of great wealth is the inevitable *claque* of insincere friends.

CLERISY *n.* (KLER uh see) the intelligencia

Public broadcasting is not intended for the public but rather the *clerisy* and their offspring.

COCKALORUM *n.* (kahk uh LOH ruhm) a small man with a big opinion of himself; bragging

The professor could only be called a *cockalorum* because his diminutive size was only surpassed by his enormous ego.

With only one victory under his belt, the novice boxer's crowing *cockalorum* was starting to grate on the champion who ended the upstart's career with one punch.

QUICK QUIZ #10

Match each word in the first column with its definition in the second column. Check your answers in the back.

1. chattel	a. painting style with light and dark
2. chiaroscuro	b. braggadocio
3. chirr	c. harsh sound
4. chthonic	d. loud
5. cincture	e. daily
6. circadian	f. enclosure
7. clamant	g. literati
8. claque	h. sycophants
9. clerisy	i. related to netherworld
10. cockalorum	j. slave

CODEX *n.* (KOH deks) a volume in manuscript, esp. an ancient one

A volume from Leonardo's notebooks is usually ascribed the name of its owner; therefore, the Hammer *Codex*, which was sold to Bill Gates, becomes the Gates *Codex*.

CODICIL *n.* (KAHD uh suhl) an appendix, esp. to a will

After her son's destructive behavior, she called her lawyer and added a *codicil* to the will.

COEVAL *adj.* (koh EE vuhl) or (KOH ee vuhl) from the same period or era; *n.* a contemporary

The prevailing theory is that the development of speech is *coeval* with the development of mankind.

Old Ms. Haberblad is jokingly referred to by the rest of the staff as being *coeval* with Moses.

COFFLE *n.* (KAWF fuhl) a group of animals or prisoners chained in a line

The lone cowboy appeared on the ridge silhouetted against the azure sky, a *coffle* of horses behind him.

COGNITIVE *adj.* (KAHG nuhd iv) or (KAHG nuh tiv) of or related to conscious thought or intellectual activity

Cognitive actions include thinking, reasoning, remembering and imagining. They are usually contrasted to affective (emotional) and conative actions (actions derived from desire). Every instinctive action can be related to these three processes. When cognitive is used in the phrase "cognitive dissonance," it refers to anxiety resulting from inconsistencies between belief and action.

Although the tests proved his *cognitive* abilities were destroyed by the overdose of heroin, he was still a remarkably talented musician.

Many of the psychological disorders that were found in returning Vietnam veterans stemmed from the *cognitive* dissonance they suffered while killing people in a war that they believed was unjust.

COGNOSCENTE *n.* (kahn yoh SHEN tee) or (kah gnuh SHEN tee) a connoisseur; one with refined taste, esp. in the fine arts.

> Van Gogh was ignored by the *cognoscenti* of his day and died a pauper.
> Despite the hoopla surrounding the exhibition, it was only attended by dealers, reviewers, and other *cognoscenti* of painting.

COLOPHON *n.* (KAHL uh fuhn) or (KAHL uh fahn) an inscription on the last page of a book telling about its publication; a publisher's trademark placed on the title page of a book

> She had found an entire first edition of *Cat's Cradle* from title-page to *colophon* in a trashcan outside her home.

COMITY *n.* (KAHM uhd ee) or (KAHM uh tee) courtesy, civility

> This word is sometimes used in the phrase "comity of nations" to describe the good will between nations that respect each other's laws and customs.
> Through diplomatic skill and deft political maneuvering, Senator Denneky was able to encourage a spirit of *comity* in all the Senate's proceedings.

COMMOVE *v.* (kuh MOOV) or (kah MOOV) to agitate; to move violently

> We *commoved* bananas, strawberries, sugar, lime juice, ice, and rum for a refreshing summer drink.

COMPORT *v.* (kuhm POHRT) to behave (oneself) in a particular manner; to agree; to suit

> Considering the dire situation in which our hero found herself, she *comported* herself with courage and dignity, refraining from all but the quietest whimper for help.
> His obsequious attitude *comports* with the image many have of poor people.
> Such a lopsided victory does not *comport* with our understanding of the phrase "athletic contest."

Quick Quiz #11

Match each word in the first column with its definition in the second column. Check your answers in the back.

1. codex	a. appendix of will
2. codicil	b. conscious thought
3. coeval	c. agitate
4. coffle	d. group chained in line
5. cognitive	e. volume
6. cognoscenti	f. contemporary
7. colophon	g. connoisseur
8. comity	h. ourtesy
9. commove	i. behave
10. comport	j. publisher's trademark

CONATION *n.* (koh NAY shun) The desire or will to perform conscious acts

Conation does not depend upon an understanding of what might cause an action. In psychology, the word is usually contrasted to cognition and affection.

The sour smelling man on the subway had a *conation* to stand up suddenly and repeat a phrase over and over again until the rest of the people in the car all spit at him in unison.

CONCUBINAGE *n.* (kahn KYOO buh nij) in law; living together while unmarried

As more Americans cohabitate not legally married, a good word needs to be developed to describe such couples. This, unfortunately, is not the word, but may be the best available description until a new word is coined. Concubinate comes from concubine which is based on roots meaning "to lie together," but the word concubine retains a negative connotation.

In ancient times in some societies, *concubinage*, while not as respected as marriage, did have the legal force of a common-law marriage.

Although members of the clergy were forbidden from marriage in the nineteenth century, the practice of *concubinage* was widespread, and led to many "illegitimate" children.

CONCUPISCENCE *n.* (kahn KYOO puhs suhns) strong desire, usually sexual desire

This word was used by the scholastic philosophers of the middle ages to refer to a longing that the soul has for sensual pleasures. It is now used more prosaicly to describe any strong desire and especially salacious lust.

Whenever the young acolyte felt *concupiscence*, he would strip off his shirt and whip himself.

All the cold showers in the world would do nothing to cool his *concupiscence*.

CONDIGN *adj.* (kuhn DYEN) deserved; appropriate

Condign is almost exclusively used to refer to punishment. A condign punishment is one that is appropriate for the crime committed.

Those who are in favor of the death penalty argue that it is a *condign* punishment for murder.

Although it was painful to have my knuckles rapped, it was certainly not *condign* censure for my heinous act of burning down the teacher's home.

CONFABULATE *v.* (kuhn FAB yuh layt) to chat; in psychology, to replace fact with fantasy in memory

After ducking away from the *confabulating* drones at the society party, our heroine found herself alone in a broom closet with only a dust mop for company.

In his padded cell he *confabulated* a memory of surfing the vast ocean on a long board.

CONSANGUINITY *n.* (kahn san GWIN et ee) or (KAHN san gwin et ee) related by blood; a close affinity

Consanguinity denotes a relationship by blood only. It is sometimes opposed to an affinity which refers to a relationship by marriage. Sometimes blood relations are discussed by degree of consanguinity. A brother, a grandfather, and a grandson might all be considered in the second degree of consanguinity. Consanguinity can also refer to a close connection or affinity.

Although surface details may vary, there is a strong *consanguinity* of all religions; religious wars are just another form of sibling rivalry.

CONTRADISTINCTION *n.* (kahn truh di STINK shun) distinction by opposite

This word is usually used in the phrase "in contradistinction to," and it indicates that two concepts are not distinguishable, but also direct opposites.

His grand ideals were in *contradistinction* to his lowly origins.

CONTRAINDICATE *v.* (kahn truh IN duh kayt) to suggest that something is inadvisable (usually used in discussing medical treatments)

Recent evidence suggests that while heavy drinking *contraindicates* pregnancy, a little wine here or there might not be dangerous.

The side effects produced by AZT do not always *contraindicate* its usefulness in fighting AIDS.

CONTUMACIOUS *adj.* (kahn tuh MAY shuhs) extremely insubordinate; rebellious

The victims most likely to receive punishment during the Inquisition were the *contumacious* ones that did not give in and admit their alleged heresies.

CONURBATION *n.* (kahn uhr BAY shun) a metropolitan area; a region that is predominantly urban

Over half of the population of the United States is concentrated in the twenty five largest *conurbations*.

It is hard to tell where the *conurbation* of New York City ends and that of Philadelphia begins.

QUICK QUIZ #12

Match each word in the first column with its definition in the second column. Check your answers in the back.

1. conation	a. appropriate
2. concubinage	b. lust
3. concupiscence	c. rebellious
4. condign	d. cohabitation
5. confabulate	e. metropolitan area
6. consanguinity	f. will
7. contradistinction	g. related
8. contraindicate	h. antithesis
9. contumacious	i. chat
10. conurbation	j. hurt

COQUET v. (koh KET) to flirt; to dally

This word comes from the French word for cock, and connotes the strutting and amorous behavior one would expect from this barnyard animal. The word "coquette" (a noun) refers to a woman who is a flirt.

She was surprised to find that she had the courage to *coquet* with many of the men at the party.

The pretty *coquette* avoided his glance, so he coughed and mussed up his hair in order to get her attention.

CORDIFORM adj. (KOH duh fohrm) shaped like a heart

Although she was trying to be polite, she couldn't help but stare at the enormous *cordiform* birthmark on his pale, hairy chest.

CORTEGE n. (KAWR tezh) a retinue; a group of attendants (sometimes spelled cortège)

First came a corps of bugles, followed by the King of England and a *cortege*of attendants.

CORUSCATE v. (KOH uh skayt) to glitter or sparkle; to be brilliant in technique or intelligence

The building burst into flame (causing untold millions of dollars in damages) but our hero could only stare incredulously at the brilliant, *corruscating* light of the fireball.

COUVADE n. (koo VAHD) A custom in certain non-Western cultures in which the husband lies in bed and performs some of the actions usually associated with a pregnant woman

Couvade syndrome is used to describe the empathetic symptoms that many men experience during their wives' pregnancies. The word comes from a French word meaning "to hatch," but the use of the word in its modern sense might have been formed due to a mistranslation of the French phrase "faire la couvade" that means loosely "to sit at home and avoid the action." Some estimate that up to 65 percent of men suffer from couvade syndrome, experiencing at least some of their partner's symptoms.

Marco Polo chronicled the practice of *couvade* in the West Yunnan province of China.

COXCOMB n. (KAHKS kohm) a fop; a self-satisfied dandy

This word usually refers to a male who is conceited and wears foppish clothing. It comes from a cock's comb (the fleshy crest of a cock). This crest looks a lot like the typical court fool's hat, and it began to be used, by association, to refer to a fool.

It was unfortunate that the great artist was a *coxcomb*, unwilling to wear any color except black and unable to talk about anything except himself.

CRAPULOUS adj. (KRAP yuh luhs) gluttonous or immoderate in drinking; suffering from the effects of overindulgence

He was a *crapulous* old man, and had he been thinking, he wouldn't have eaten that last wafer-thin mint.

After the all-night fête to celebrate his graduation, he succumbed to a *crapulous* slumber.

CRAQUELURE *n.* (kra KLOOR) fine cracks that appear on oil paintings

This word refers to those fine cracks that appear on old oil paintings, but the word can sometimes be used figuratively to describe images with the appearance of fine cracks.

The art historian seemed oblivious to the artistic expression of the paintings, instead he concerned himself with the degree of *craquelure* on each piece.

Simone O'Calla's bald pate was translucent, with a *craquelure* of blue upon her fine skin.

CREPITATE *v.* (KREP uh tayt) to make a crackling noise; to crackle

On his way to a midnight snack of leftover meatloaf, our hero was given away when the joints in his knees *crepitated*, waking up the entire household.

The instant after the bomb hit the tower, every radio in the city began to *crepitate*, ending the inhabitants' ability to hear the State's viewpoint of the recent events.

CREPUSCULAR *adj.* (kruh PUHS kyuh luhr) of or like twilight, dim; active during twilight (zoological)

Sometimes when the word is used figuratively, it can imply the breaking dawn, a period of as yet incomplete enlightenment.

She strained to see his barely visible silhouette in the *crepuscular* light.

The development of the Babylonian legal system, while set in stone by the code of Hamurabbi, occurred during that *crepuscular* period of history when little was saved for posterity.

Quick Quiz #13

Match each word in the first column with its definition in the second column. Check your answers in the back.

1.	coquet	a.	man acts pregnant
2.	cordiform	b.	dandy
3.	cortege	c.	glitter
4.	coruscate	d.	heart shaped
5.	couvade	e.	flirt
6.	coxcomb	f.	of twilight
7.	crapulous	g.	retinue
8.	craquelure	h.	cracks on oil paintings
9.	crepitate	i.	overindulgence
10.	crepuscular	j.	crackle

CROTCHET *n.* (KRAHCH uht) an unusual or whimsical fancy; a peculiar trick or dodge; *adj.* crotchety (KRAHCH uhd ee)

He was an iconoclast, full of absurd crotchets, but when it came to his dinner, all he would eat was meat and potatoes.

One generation's crotchets become the next generation's truisms.

CUCKOLD *n.* (KUHK uhld) a derisive word for a man whose wife is unfaithful; to make into a cuckold

Cuckold comes from the French word cucuault which in turn comes from cuckoo, the cuckoo bird. Some of these birds have the habit of laying their eggs in another bird's nest, so that the baby cuckoo will be taken care of by the unsuspecting mother bird. From this idea came the sense that cuckoo's were somehow unfaithful, and the word has come to English to mean a husband who has been cheated on. Cuckquean, which derisively describes a woman who has been cheated on by her husband, is obsolete. This is unfortunate, because one could have said that a woman had been made cuckquean by a coxcomb.

CUNCTATION *n.* (kuhnk TAY shun) procrastination

Despite her proclivity for *cunctation,* she finished the application on time.

After more than a decade of *cunctation,* he finally got around to cleaning the refrigerator.

CUPIDITY *n.* (kyoo PID uhd ee) excessive greed or avarice, covetousness

Cupidity stresses the intensity of the desire for wealth or another's possessions. It differs from greed in that greed refers to a lust that is a controlling passion. A greedy person is obsessed with another's possessions or wealth and is also a bit nasty. One with cupidity need not necessarily be mean. A poor person might feel cupidity in the presence of great wealth, but greed implies a desire for something that is not needed.

The riches of the Arawak Indians were an object of *cupidity* for the arriving European powers.

CYNOSURE *n.* (SYE nuh shoor) an object at the focal point of attention; something that is used as a guide

This word comes from the Greek word kynosoura (dog's tail) used to describe the constellation ursa minor where the North Star is located. From this, the word came to mean anything that serves as a guide.

The recently-blonde Lisa Evangelist, the *cynosure* of the party, was surrounded by a retinue of hair-dressers and make-up artists.

During its early years, the newly-formed security council of the United Nations was the *cynosure* of the peaceful hopes of the entire world.

DADA *n.* (DAH dah) a literary and artistic movement (1916-1923) in Europe that thrived on absurdity, flouting conventional artistic values

The word dada comes from the French word for hobby horse, an arbitrarily chosen symbol for the movement. An early review was entitled *Être Sur Son Dada,* (ride one's hobby-horse) and the name continued to be used to describe the movement.

For many, the creations of the *Dada* period were a complete repudiation of their deeply held aesthetic beliefs.

Her new film was the greatest expression of *dadaism* since the twenties.

DAEDAL *adj.* (DEE duhl) ingeniously formed, intricate or complex; finely made and ingenious in design. This word is related to the Greek Daedalus, who in mythology was the constructor of the labyrinth and the maker of the wings which his son Icarus wore when flying too close to the sun.

After winding his way through the *daedal* system of trains, busses, and subways that serve as an inexpensive way to get around the city of New York, our hero found himself flummoxed by a simple ticket vending machine.

Multimedia, in the hands of a skillful practitioner, can make concepts accessible in a *daedal* fashion.

DALLIANCE *n.* (DAL lee uhns) playful flirtation; frivolous action

Although on its surface it appeared harmless, his flirtation with Maureen was much more than a gentle *dalliance*.

Even after the conspirator received his mission, he continued to spend much of his time in idle *dalliance*.

DASEIN *n.* (DAH zyen) a philosophical term for existence or being

To bring something into dasein is to give it existence within the spatiotemporal realm.

While Descartes could put it simply—Cogito ergo sum (I think, therefore, I am)—Hegel might say that I am *dasein*, i.e. empirically here.

DAUPHIN *n.* (DAW fuhn) the eldest son of the King of France (fourteenth to nineteenth century)

All of France celebrated with the announcement of the birth of the new *dauphin*.

To extend her powers, the queen of Scotland began a dalliance with the young *dauphin*, that ended in her becoming both Queen of Scotland and Queen of France.

QUICK QUIZ #14

Match each word in the first column with its definition in the second column. Check your answers in the back.

1. crotchet		a.	intricate
2. cuckold		b.	nonsense
3. cunctation		c.	procrastination
4. cupidity		d	existence
5. cynosure		e.	whimsical notion
6. dada		f.	focal point
7. daedal		g.	covetousness
8. dalliance		h.	cheated on man
9. dasein		i.	eldest son of King of France
10. dauphin		j.	flirtation

DECALOGUE *n.* (DEK uh lawg) the Ten Commandments; a set of rules that is fundamental

Upon seeing the Israelites worshipping the golden calf in the desert, Moses cast down the two tablets of the *Decalogue*, shattering them into a million pieces.

DÉCLASSÉ *adj.* (day kluh SAY) having reduced social status, of inferior status; one with reduced social status

Formerly *déclassé*, fake fur in brilliant colors has been making a comeback among a certain set.

Formerly a superpower, England is now treated as a *déclassé*, forced to kowtow to its former colonies.

DECOLLATE *v.* (duh KAH layt) to behead

The guillotine sliced through the air instantly *decollating* the former King of France.

DÉCOLLETAGE *n.* (day kah luh TAHZH) a neckline on a dress cut low to show off shoulders; exposure of said shoulders

The adjective form is décolleté (day kah luh TAY) which can also be used figuratively to express the idea of a woman who might wear a décolleté dress.

Attached to the *décolletage* were a glittering stream of brilliant rhinestones.

We were a bit surprised by her ever increasing *décolletage*, but ascribed it to her desire to be comfortable during the heat of summer.

DECONSTRUCTION *n.* (dee cahn STRUHK shun) a system of literary criticism in which a work of art is examined to extract hidden meanings that may not have been the author's intention

Deconstruction, a method of criticism that has been popular on college campuses in the seventies and eighties assumes that there is no single meaning in any work of art, that a piece can be broken down (deconstructed) to show a myriad of meanings. Several methods are used: a critique might compare a work to others by the same artist, analyze internal contradictions, look at an artist's socioeconomic background, look at other information (interviews and such) about the artist, and compare anything found with the actual language used by a writer.

At its best, deconstructionism allows for a more complex understanding of a work of art. At its worst, it obliterates the role of the artist, denying her ability to fulfill any of her original intentions in making art.

"To locate the promising marginal text, to disclose the undecidable moment, to pry it loose with the positive lever of the signifier; to reverse the resident hierarchy, only to displace it; to dismantle in order to reconstitute what is always already inscribed. *Deconstruction* in a nutshell."

—G. C. Spivak

DEFALCATE *v.* (duh FAL kayt) to embezzle

Originally derived from the French word for sickle, defalcate used to mean to curtail or reduce, but this meaning has disappeared and the word now means to misappropriate funds held in one's care.

A determined clerk can defalcate more money than even the most brazen bank-robber.

DEFENESTRATION *n.* (dee fen uh STRAY shun) the act of tossing someone or something out a window

That such a sesquipedalian word would be coined to describe such an undistinguished event is no accident. On May 21, 1618 in a prelude to the Thirty Years War, Bohemian insurgents threw two Imperial commissioners and a secretary out a window. This action became known as the "defenestration of Prague," which helped bring this term into common usage.

They met for the first time during the great fire of 1983 when he threw her out a three story window. After this awkward *defenestration*, a courtship that would lead to marriage commenced.

DÉGAGÉ *adj.* (day gah ZHAY) casual, relaxed

After having casually defenestrated the neighborhood bully, our hero adopted a *dégagé* pose when confronted by the bully's brother.

The fashion world was rebelling against the strict conformity of the eighties by producing *dégagé* suits with wavy lines.

DEGAUSS *v.* (dee GAOOS) to eliminate the magnetic field of something

One of many inventions perfected by the military, degaussing involves using an electronic current surrounding a metallic ship to prevent it from being blown up by magnetic mines.

Before recording, most VCR's *degauss* the tape heads to ensure proper operation.

DEISM *n.* (DEE iz uhm) The belief that God created the universe and then left it to its own devices

An adherent of deism believes that God is the divine watchmaker, that after creating the universe, God abandoned it and has not intervened supernaturally in human affairs. This rationalistic movement was developed by John Locke (1632–1704) and believed that only through a study of nature can God be understood.

He always said that if he had to pick a religion, it would be *deism*. It wasn't as if he was an atheist—he believed in God—he just felt that all of organized religion was hogwash.

Quick Quiz #15

Match each word in the first column with its definition in the second column. Check your answers in the back.

1. Decalogue
2. déclassé
3. decollate
4. décolletage
5. deconstruction
6. defalcate
7. defenestration
8. dégagé
9. degauss
10. deism

a. embezzle
b. neckline
c. system of philosophy that assumes nothing
d. inferior
e. demagnetise
f. throw out a window
g. divine watchmaker
h. behead
i. ten commandments
j. casual

DELIQUESCE *v.* (DEL uh KWES) to melt away, to become liquid

Although this word is normally used in the sciences to describe biological or chemical phenomena, it is also repeatedly used in a humorous fashion as a fancy way of saying "liquefy."

"Lips parted in ecstasy, *deliquescing* lipsticks, glistening buttocks and anatomical displays not suitable for discussion in a family newspaper occupy rectangular areas placed off-center on large metal panels of the type used by sign painters."
—Pepe Karmel, *The New York Times*

DELPHIAN *adj.* (DEL fee uhn) of or related to the oracle at Delphi in Greek mythology; oracular, prophetic but obscure (sometimes delphic (DEL fik))

This word's primary meaning describes the Delphian oracle of Apollo where many ancients asked questions and received obscure answers. The oracle was discovered when goatherds noticed that a certain spot on the slopes of the mountain Parnassus caused their goats to go into convulsions. They assumed it was some type of vapor, and one goatherd thought it might be fun to give it a try and began spouting out incoherent ramblings which his brethren assumed to be prophetic. A temple was built, a priestess assigned, and the rest is history. Used today, *delphian* suggests something that is prophetic but exceedingly difficult to understand.

The *delphic* response from the Magic Eight Ball neither confirmed nor denied the wisdom of quitting her job before finding a new one.

DEMARCHE *n.* (day MAHRSH) course of action; a diplomatic initiative or countermove; a statement made to a public official by citizens

Although we thought our most recent *demarche* clever, our enemy caught on right away and was waiting for us with guns drawn.

Civil rights workers made a *demarche* to JFK asking him for help in ending the terrorism perpetuated by the KKK.

DEMESNE *n.* (duh MAYN) (law) possessed legally; land attached to a home or estate; a region; a realm

The legal meaning of this word, to possess legally, is different from the idea of ownership. Someone who rents from an owner is said to hold his land in demesne.

After the Civil War, Scarlett O'Hara was only able to keep her family home and its *demesne*; the rest had to be sold to the hated Northerners to keep from starving.

Still seeking universal truth, she was dismayed to find that the *demesne* of knowledge was so broad.

DEMIMONDE *n.* (de mee MAHND) a class of kept women or other woman of lower social standing; a group with marginal success or respectability

This word comes from the French demi (half) and monde (world) and signifies something outside the accepted realm of respectability.

A former princess, she was now relegated to cavorting with the *demimonde* of the Latin quarter in Paris.

DESIDERATE *v.* (duh SID uh rayt) to seek earnestly, to express a desire for, to miss

Among the items the populace desiderated were good jobs, homes in the suburbs, and the end of welfare as we know it.

Maurice *desiderated* a life that he knew he could not afford, so he did what every young American college graduate did . . . he overused his credit cards and bought a yacht.

DESUETUDE *n.* (DES wee tood) a state of being unused or abandoned

This word is constructed from the root "suecere" (to become accustomed). Other words from this root are consuetude (KAHN swuh tood) (custom or usage) and mansuetude (MAN swuh tood) (mildness; tameness).

After many years of desuetude, freight trains have recently been given much more of a role in our transportation system.

The conservative members of the senate foresee total desuetude of our society as we know it should taxes rise even a small percentage.

The burnt-out shell of a brownstone would require years of work to keep it from falling into desuetude.

DETERIORISM *n.* (duh TIR ee uh riz uhm) the belief that things tend toward the worst

Deteriorism is the opposite of agathism and meliorism; one who adheres to its philosophy feels that the world is deteriorating.

Although the papers declared the comet a harbinger of good times, my uncle, a *deteriorist*, believes that it presaged the worst.

DETERMINISM *n.* (duh TUHR muh niz uhm) the philosophy that everything is caused by some previous action that is out of human hands

Determinism can be broken down further into ethical determinism, cosmological determinism, and theological determinism. Ethical determinism refers to the idea that all acts are controlled by previous actions and that free will is essentially an illusion. Cosmological determinism implies that all of nature is determined by antecedent causes. Theological determinism is the belief in predestination.

DETRITUS *n.* (duh TRYED uhs) the loose material wearing away from rocks; any product of wearing away, a fragment

The erosion to the Colorado River produced a canyon and various deposits of misshapen *detritus* that impeded any rescue attempt.

His admirers may have felt the novel a bit unoriginal, but his critics recognized it as the *detritus* of a previous novel.

QUICK QUIZ #16

Match each word in the first column with its definition in the second column. Check your answers in the back.

1. deliquesce
2. delphian
3. demarche
4. demesne
5. demimonde
6. desiderate
7. desuetude
8. deteriorism
9. determinism
10. detritus

a. maneuver
b. netherworld
c. unused
d. everything is caused
e. desire
f. rubble
g. obscurely prophetic
h. pessimism
i. melt away
j. domain

DEVOLUTION *n.* (dev uh LOO shun) descent through stages of a process; transfer of rights to a successor; a transfer of power from central to local government; decentralization

The recent attempts by Congress to give power to the states from the federal government is referred to as *devolution*.

Henry held on, somewhere in the chasm between life and death, making it impossible to begin the *devolution* of the crown to his son.

DEWY-EYED *adj.* (DOO wee eyed) naive

The "dewy" of "dewy eyed" refers to the untouched quality of dew. Someone who is dewy or dewy eyed is an innocent boy or an ingenue.

He entered the school *dewy-eyed* and left it jaded.

Although she appeared *dewy-eyed*, she had been through much in her life and was not to be fooled by such an old con.

DHARMA *n.* (DAHR muh) the principle that orders the universe; one's conduct with regard to that principle; something's essential function

Dharma is the true meaning or essential function of the Universe, but in Hinduism the word refers to one's duty to one's caste. In Buddhism it refers to the teachings of Buddha. The written explanation of his rules is called "the word" while the entire system is called "dharma."

It is the *dharma* of a king to rule, just as it is the dharma of a cow to graze, a cheetah to run, or of water to be wet.

DIACRITICAL *adj.* (DYE uh krit ik uhl) serving to separate, distinguishing; able to discriminate

Heard most often in reference to marks that appear on top of vowels to indicate particular sounds. This word is also used to mean "distinctive" or "discerning."

The *diacritical* elements in his paintings were the sharp gashes made in the canvas by a meat cleaver. The tattered remains of the stretched canvas were often sold for the price of a small bungalow in Massachusetts.

DIADEM *n.* (DYE uh dem) a crown that symbolizes royalty; royal power; *v.* to adorn with a diadem

This word originally described the royal headbands of Persian kings that Alexander of Macedon wore when he wanted to look regal. It is now more often used in a general sense to describe a crown or royal power.

I realized the drawing of Philip of Macedon looked vaguely athletic, because his *diadem* looked like a sweatband.

DIAPHANOUS *adj.* (dye A fuh nuhs) perfectly transparent or translucent; airy; insubstantial

The *diaphanous* ice due to the sudden freeze gave the ice fishermen a perfect view of the refulgent goldfish.

She peered through the *diaphanous* veil of her wedding dress and saw the groom kick up his heels and sprint out of the church.

The schizophrenic's *diaphanous* delusions of glory swiftly gave way to the dregs of despair.

DIASPORA *n.* (dye AS puh ruh) the breaking up of the Jewish Community in the sixth century when they were exiled from Israel to Babylon; Jewish communities outside Israel; any dispersion of a people with a common origin

The word "diaspora" originates from a phrase in Deuteronemy of the Old Testament. It was foretold that the Jews "shalt be a Diaspora (or dispersion) in all kingdoms of the earth."

It was a relief for the wandering Armenian to come upon a neighborhood of the Armenian *diaspora* in Brooklyn.

DIDDLE *v.* (DID uhl) to cheat or swindle (slang); to masturbate; to copulate

Although he was known for his ability to con multi-national corporations, he would not *diddle* one of his own workers.

DINGLE *n.* (DIN guhl) a small, wooded valley

The heath grew a different color in a solitary *dingle* north of Lancaster.

DIPHTHONG *n.* (DIF thawn) a single syllable made by combining two vowels

A diphthong is made when two vowels are combined so that the sounds glide from one to the other. Boy, for example, consists of the diphthong between the 'o' sound and the 'ee' sound.

"You look like a COW!" she said, putting special emphasis on the *diphthong*, "take that ring out of your nose."

QUICK QUIZ #17

Match each word in the first column with its definition in the second column. Check your answers in the back.

1. devolution	a.	wooded valley
2. dewy-eyed	b.	dispersion of Jews
3. dharma	c.	decentralization
4. diacritical	d.	aieee
5. diadem	e.	naive
6. diaphanous	f.	primary principle
7. Diaspora	g.	distinguishing
8. diddle	h.	crown
9. dingle	i.	translucent
10. diphthong	j.	to cheat

DIRIGIBLE *adj.* (DIR uh juh buhl) able to be directed; *n.* a flying ship (such as a blimp)

As the Wizard's gaudily painted balloon drifted over the ocean, Dorothy was surprised to find out that it was not *dirigible*.

Because the Hindenburg exploded in front of thirty journalists, many photos were taken of the burning *dirigible*.

DISABUSE *v.* (DIS uh byooz) to correct someone; to free from misconception

His first attempts at *disabusing* me were a complete disaster, but eventually I was convinced that love was not a bowl of cherries.

Disabused of his grand illusions, the tramp shuffled along, tearing up his winning lottery ticket.

DISCOMBOBULATE *v.* (dis kuhm BAHB yuh layt) to confuse; to throw into a state of chaos or confusion

After being hit on the head by the frying pan, Peter was so *discombobulated* that he left his coat in the kitchen.

DISSONANCE *n.* (DIS suh nuhns) a combination of sounds that is harsh; discord; discrepancy; strife

An easy way to produce *dissonance* on a piano is to hit a note and its flatted fifth. Such a sound grates on the ears.

He could not believe that their nubile ears were not hurt by such *dissonance*, but the mirthful dancers showed no sign of pain.

The *dissonance* caused by the beautiful strains of Beethoven's *Ninth Symphony* in juxtaposition to the violence of the movie *Die Hard* produced a mind-boggling effect on the audience.

DISTAFF *adj.* (DIH staf) relating to a woman; relating to a female genetic line

A distaff was originally a tool used in spinning wool, a job that was usually done by women. Over time, the word was used to symbolize woman's work and then to mean "womanly" or "related to a woman."

She could trace her ancestry from the *distaff* side all the way back to Moses, but her father was of uncertain origin.

Cheryl Miller's elegant shooting touch is the *distaff* equivalant of her brother's stroke.

DITHER *n.* (DITH uhr) a state of nervous indecisiveness; *v.* to act with confusion or indecision

Expecting an empty house, his fiancée was thrown into a *dither* by the crowd of well-wishers and drunkards living at his home.

While the lame duck congress *dithered* over pay raises, their constituents became incensed, and riots occurred over much of the United States.

DIVA *n.* (DEE vuh) an opera singer; a prima donna

From the Italian word for "goddess," a diva is a distinguished opera singer.

The cognoscenti at the Opera house could not contain their glee when the latest *diva* approached the wings to enter the stage.

After performing the most famous of all arias from *The Magic Flute*, the *diva* collapsed in fatigue and was carried off the stage in a piano crate.

DIVAGATE *v.* (DEE vuh gayt) to wander; to digress

Their discussion *divagated* from love to murder and then back again.

Just as an autumn leaf *divagates* to the ground, his opinion of her shifted one way and the next.

DOCENT *adj.* (DOH suhnt) serving to instruct; *n.* in some universities, a teacher who is not a member of the regular faculty; a tour guide in a museum or cathedral

The *docent* authority of the Catholic church has recently been questioned by those who want their children to learn about contraception.

Although any fool could see that it was one of Picasso's lesser works, the *docent* blathered on about its expressive powers as the dilettantes absorbed every word.

DOGGEREL *n.* (DAWG ruhl) crudely constructed poetry or verse (usually humorous) (also doggrel)

It seemed pure torture to me to make those school children read such vile *doggerel*.

QUICK QUIZ #18

Match each word in the first column with its definition in the second column. Check your answers in the back.

1. dirigible		a.	undeceive
2. disabuse		b.	wander
3. discombobulate		c.	discord
4. dissonance		d.	tour guide
5. distaff		e.	crude poetry
6. dither		f.	blimp
7. diva		g.	confuse
8. divagate		h.	female
9. docent		i.	agitated indecisiveness
10. doggerel		j.	opera singer

DOLOR *n.* (DOH luhr) grief, sorrow

The death of her firstborn left her in a state of *dolor* and despair that persisted until her death.

DONNISH *adj.* (DAH nish) like a university don; bookish; pedantic

He had an annoyingly *donnish* way of correcting her most minute faults, while he could commit a gross offense without fearing censure.

DONNYBROOK *n.* (DAH nee brook) a tempestuous brawl

Donnybrook is the name of a suburb of Dublin once known for its riotous annual fair; the word is still used to describe a free-for-all.

It would have been disingenuous of them to have been surprised by the intellectual *donnybrook* created by *The Bell Curve*, a book that declared differences of intelligence to be genetically determined.

The introduction of the articles of impeachment created a *donnybrook* in the normally placid House of Representatives.

DORMITION *n.* (dawr MIS shun) death that resembles sleep

The cardinal was lying still, appearing to sleep, but it was *dormition*.

Martin was forced to attend a series of lectures so boring that he prayed for *dormition*.

DORSAL *adj.* (DAWR suhl) of the back or upper part of an organism

The little boy grabbed Flipper's *dorsal* fin and was pulled away from the attacking sharks.

An airhole was found on the dorsal of the creature, but it is unlikely that it was used for breathing.

DOWAGER *n.* (DOW uh jeur) a widow with a title or property inherited from her husband; an older woman of high social standing

By marrying her *dowager* aunt, he hoped to gad about as he had before, but instead he fell for the niece who was promptly disinherited.

The *dowagers* clucked their tongues at the lack of respect shown them by the upstart debutantes.

DOYENNE *n.* (DOI uhn) the senior female member of a group; the senior male member of a group is called a doyen.

She felt intimidated when introduced to Stein, the *doyenne* of the lost generation, but was taken aback by her warmth and good humor.

In twenty years, Thomas will be the *doyen* among Supreme Court justices, but until then, he has much to learn before gaining the respect heaped upon Marshall.

DUCTILE *n.* (DUHK tuhl) malleable

Although copper's *ductile* nature makes it perfect for wire, it is a bad substance for making a sword or a tool. For this reason, the invention of bronze went a long way toward the creation of civilization.

The laws set forth in the Constitution have proved to be exceedingly *ductile* and accommodating to vast social and political changes in the United States.

A good politician is able to convince the *ductile* multitude of anything. His problems arise when he is faced with an opponent who can do the same.

DUDGEON *n.* (DUH juhn) sour, angry or indignant mood

Dudgeon is almost exclusively used with 'in' and a qualifying adjective. (e.g. in high dudgeon)

After the humiliating comment made by the chairman, she slammed the door and flew off in high *dudgeon*.

He broke all of her crayons from payne's gray to Turkish purple and left her fuming in high *dudgeon*.

DULCET *adj.* (DUHL suht) melodious, having a nice agreeable sound; soothing

Dulcet comes from the Latin "dulcis" which means "sweet," and it used to have a general meaning, but today the word is most often used to describe sounds.

Although some found them obnoxious, the computer consultant found the noises made by his modem *dulcet*.

Anon out of the earth a Fabrick huge
Rose like an Exhalation, with the sound
Of *Dulcet* Symphonies and voices sweet,
—from *Paradise Lost*, by John Milton

QUICK QUIZ #19

Match each word in the first column with its definition in the second column. Check your answers in the back.

1. dolor	a. sorrow
2. donnish	b. pedantic
3. donnybrook	c. widow with husband's money
4. dormition	d. senior member
5. dorsal	e. melodious
6. dowager	f. malleable
7. doyenne	g. brawl
8. ductile	h sleep of death
9. dudgeon	i. rear
10. dulcet	j. angry mood

DYAD *n.* (DYE ad) two individuals thought of as a pair

A dyad is used in sociology to describe a pair that maintains a significant relationship.

Historian Gilbert Bertrude noticed a *dyadic* relationship between form and content that allowed any artistic movement to be explored by using modernistic tendencies.

DYBBUK *n.* (DI buhk) the soul of a dead person that controls a living person's behavior

This word, from Jewish folklore, comes from a Hebrew word meaning "to cleave."

Rachel thought that control by a *dybbuk* was the only explanation for his bizarre actions, but her family seemed to think that he was just plain meshugene.

She petitioned the Rabbi for help in removing this *dybbuk*, but he refused, arguing that in the twentieth century, one should see a crazy-doctor, before a rabbi, to exorcise such demons.

DYSPEPTIC *adj.* (Duh SPEP tik) having dyspepsia (dis SPEP shuh), a digestive disorder characterized by gas, nausea, and a feeling of fullness; having a gloomy disposition

The second meaning is derived from the first. Someone with dyspepsia would certainly not be in a good mood.

Maurice took a *dyspeptic* view of the burgeoning friendship between his mother and Ross Limbergh.

ECCE HOMO *n.* (e chay HOH moh) an image of Jesus wearing a crown of thorns

Ecce homo means literally "Behold the man!" and comes from the words that Pilate allegedly said when Jesus appeared before the Jews wearing a crown of thorns.

To ensure a swift trip to heaven, the Mafioso bought one *ecce homo* for every ton of cocaine that he sold to the black market.

ÉCLAT *n.* (ay KLAHT) brilliant success; acclaim; brilliance in performance or achievement

Coming from an old French word meaning to splinter, to explode, this word has become part of the English language meaning brilliance.

Maude dominated student government with *éclat*, winning passage for any law that she deemed important.

His ambitious performance was given far more *éclat* than it deserved.

ECUMENICAL *adj.* (ek uyh MEN eh kuhl) universal, of worldwide scope; related to the world-wide Catholic church

Afraid of its possible effect on *ecumenical* trade, the United States declined to enter the war in the Balkans.

While he insisted on following only the rules of the Catholic religion, she advocated a more *ecumenical* approach, insisting on the celebration of Jewish, Muslim, and Buddhist holidays as well as the Christian ones.

The dispute between the missionaries and their charges had degenerated to the point where direct support from the Pope and his *ecumenical* council were required.

EDACIOUS *adj.* (ee DAY shuhs) having an insatiable appetite

Most often used in a humorous manner when describing appetite, this word is also used to describe time.

He had an *edacious* appetite and could easily consume twice his mother's weight in food a day.

The *edacious* tooth of time was gnawing away at the fortifications of the bridge, biding its time until a certain car with a passenger who had eaten too many eclairs drove by.

EDUCE *v.* (ee DYOOS) to draw out something that is present in a latent state, elicit, evoke

Although educe can sometimes be used interchangeably with such synonyms as elicit, evoke, extract, or extort, its meaning is slightly different. Educe usually means drawing something out that is latent or potential in something. Evoke, however, is used more often in describing that which arouses an emotion. One educes something from data. One uses words to evoke a feeling. Elicit is similar to evoke, but it implies a certain degree of care or trouble in drawing out.

Through using different pedagogical techniques, the tutor attempted to *educe* the students' latent desire to study.

Although the polls successfully *educed* the country's distaste for welfare, it did not discover what alternatives were popular.

EFFETE *adj.* (uh FEET) exhausted, depleted of vitality; infertile; overrefined

Effete used to describe an animal that had already borne its young, one that was worn out. It now is used in a much more general sense to describe something that has ceased to be productive.

Sharecropping on such eroded *effete* land was a losing proposition, but Nicholas had nowhere else to go and no one else to see.

Who would have known that such a virile and handsome lover would turn into an *effete* fop who could do nothing but spend his wife's money on ever-more expensive clothing.

His new work was critiqued by an *effete* group of self-important intellectuals whose moribund opinions were long-since disregarded.

EFFLUVIUM *n.* (eh FLOO vee uhm) a vapor which smells bad; a waste product; the gas given off by decaying material

From afar, the queen's coterie had a glamorous look, but at close range these apparently zaftig beauties were merely corseted fat dowagers emanating the *effluvia* of myriad perfumes applied too wantonly.

Had her sense of smell been blessedly defunct, she might have only noticed the gorgeous spectacle that surrounds Fresh Kills landfill in Staten Island. But unfortunately, she could smell the *effluvium* of decaying trash.

The chemical plant's *effluvia* seeped into the groundwater and caused the genetic mutation that gave Delphine Blue her super powers.

QUICK QUIZ #20

Match each word in the first column with its definition in the second column. Check your answers in the back.

1. dyad		a. elicit
2. dybbuk		b. depleted
3. dyspeptic		c. brilliance
4. ecce homo		d. pair
5. éclat		e. gloomy
6. ecumenical		f. universal
7. edacious		g. voracious
8. educe		h. Jesus in thorns
9. effete		i. bad smelling gas
10. effluvium		j. demon

ÉLAN *n.* (ay LAHN) enthusiasm or vigor; distinctive style

Élan is sometimes used in the phrase "élan vital" (ay LAHN vee tahl) which describes life's vital force. Philosopher Henri Bergson used the phrase to designate the fundamental creative life force that is present in all organisms.

The ballet was performed with considerable dash and *élan*, leaving the spectators breathless.

Although poor, he carried himself and his rags with such *élan*, that his tony neighbors often forgot that he lived over a heating grate.

In Mary Shelley's Frankenstein, and other books of its ilk, electricity is a kind of *élan vital*, able to give life to dead objects.

ELEEMOSYNARY *adj.* (el ee MAHS uhn ehr ee) charitable, or related to charity; given as an act of charity

Although you might not think it from looking, this word is related to the word alms, which has gone through a number of changes its earlier form of ælmysse.

"What poor people need today is not *eleemosynary* relief, but good jobs at decent wages," said the politician whose every need was taken care of by the government.

The church supported *eleemosynary* education in several poor areas.

ELISION *n.* (uh LIH zhuhn) the omission of a vowel at the end of a word for the sake of poetic measure as in "Th' embattled plain"; the act of omitting something

Many opera goers don't realize that the performances that they see are usually characterized by *elisions* of many scenes that would make them too long for today's viewers.

His concise style was not arrived at directly; a viewing of his manuscript shows that he *elided* a great deal.

EMBRANGLE *v.* (uhm BRAN guhl) to entangle; to mix up in confusion (also imbrangle)

The decision to invade Europe was *embrangled* with concepts of nationalism, sovereignty and politics.

The repeated scandals and missteps *embrangled* the President's first two years.

EMEND *v.* (ee MEND) or (uh MEND) to correct, improve, esp. to correct a literary text

The turgid text was greatly *emended* by a skilled editor who turned a crisp black and white manuscript into a sea of bloody red ink.

The author could take no credit for the plaudits received concerning his recent novel. It had been *emended* beyond recognition by an unheralded editor.

EMPIRICISM *n.* (em PIR uh siz uhm) the view that experience is the only valid source of knowledge; a way of practicing medicine in which all theory is disregarded and only practical experience is used; quackery

This word has two meanings that at first seem somewhat contradictory. The first, that experience of the senses is the only valid source of knowledge, forms the basis of the scientific method as developed by John Locke. The second meaning, however, is related to an ancient cult of physicians who disregarded any medical theory or accepted practice. The Empirici, as opposed to the Dogmatici and Methodici, drew entirely from experience, excluding philosophical theory. These physicians ignored the standards of medical "science" and were labeled quacks. But then, when you consider just how barbaric ancient medical procedures were (with bleedings and blistering and such), it is hard to imagine that empiricists were any worse than the mainstream doctors.

Relying solely upon the data derived from an *empirical* study of a soup kitchen, his research did little to explain the courses of poverty and homelessness.

ENCAUSTIC *n.* (ehn KAWS tik) a method of painting in which pigment in hot wax is fused with heat; a painting produced in this fashion

Many of Jasper Johns' paintings were produced in *encaustic*, which has great advantages. The paint doesn't crack, no matter how thick, and the final product, as long as it is kept away from heat, will last indefinitely.

ENCOMIUM *n.* (ehn KOH mee uhm) eulogy or formal expression of praise; a panegyric; warm praise

After his return to the Philippines, MacArther received an unstinting *encomium* from his junior officers.

The book, written by the president himself, was basically one long *encomium* about his achievements.

ENSCONCE *v.* (ehnz KAHNS) to settle oneself snugly; to hide or place in a secure place

Ensconced warmly in the igloo, Sam could not believe that it was thirty degrees below zero outside.

It was not surprising to see the cat *ensconced* in the laundry basket; it was the only place she could avoid the slobbering dog.

EPICENE *adj.* (EH puh seen) having characteristics of both male and female; effeminate; neuter (as in language)

From afar, the shadowy figure appeared *epicene*, but as it approached, he realized that it was a woman.

The painting was full of *epicene* forms that the artist said were all images of his mother.

The tough-looking longshoreman was really *epicene* after he removed all of his flannel.

Quick Quiz #21

Match each word in the first column with its definition in the second column. Check your answers in the back.

1. élan	a. experience is supreme
2. eleemosynary	b. mix up
3. elision	c. to sunggle
4. embrangle	d. charitable
5. emend	e. correct
6. empiricism	f. hermaphroditic
7. encaustic	g. enthusiasm
8. encomium	h. panegyric
9. ensconce	i. hot wax painting
10. epicene	j. omitting a sound

EPIGONE *n.* (EP uh gohn) an heir or imitator, usually second rate, esp. in the arts

An epigone originally referred to one of the seven sons of the seven heroes who fought valiantly at Thebes to avenge a wrong. After all but one of the seven original heroes were killed, their sons attempted the same task. The word is most often used in its plural form (epigones or epigoni) to refer to a subsequent generation of imitators.

Marx and Engels, unlike the *epigones* that followed, understood the motivations that might lead to communist agitation.

EPIPHANY *n.* (uh PIF uh nee) a manifestation of God or other divine being; a sudden understanding of the essential meaning of something

Christianity believes in the *epiphany* of God in Christ.

The answer to the puzzle came to me as an *epiphany*.

EPISTEMOLOGY *n.* (uh PIS tuh muh law jee) a philosophic study of the origin, nature and methods of knowledge, esp. concerned with limits and validity

Epistemology, as expressed by the theories of Descartes, Spinoza and Leibniz, attempted to integrate rational knowledge with a metaphysical belief in innate ideas. Unlike empiricism, which ignores all but sense experience, an epistemologist would fit sense experiences to a system of ideas already held to be true. Hence, Descartes might begin his discourses by looking at the world through an empirical mold, but finish them through applying our faith in God to existential questions.

The ultimate expression of *epistemology* is "cogito ergo sum," I think therefore, I am.

Plato is considered the first *epistemologist*; he often asked how people know what they know.

EPISTOLARY *adj.* (uh PIS tuh leh ree) relating to letters; contained in letters; written in the form of a bunch of letters

While the telephone seemed to reduce people's *epistolary* talents, increased use of e-mail has enabled many who would not normally carry on correspondence to exchange notes back and forth.

He looked forward to seeing his pen pal for the first time; their *epistolary* love affair had burgeoned over the years.

Alice Walker's *epistolary* novel chronicled the lives of two African-American sisters living on opposite sides of the world.

EPONYMOUS *adj.* (uh PAWN uh muhs) relating to a person whose name is the source of another thing (city, country, era)

She was pleased to know that her *eponymous* ancestor had founded several charitable organizations and had only been in jail once.

EQUIPOISE *n.* (EH kwuh poiz) or (EE kwuh poiz) equal in weight or relationship, equilibrium; a counterbalance

As he teetered a bit to the right, the circus star kept his left hand raised in *equipoise*, but to no avail; a gust of wind blew, and he fell to the ground.

The aristocracy, having served as an *equipoise* to the clergy, was weakened, causing the first of many church-backed attempts to grab power.

ERSATZ *adj.* (EHR zahts) an imitation, usually inferior

Even though she wore an *ersatz* fur coat made out of synthetic materials, she was still subject to the taunts of animal rights obsessives.

Due to their abject poverty, he was forced to go back to drinking an *ersatz* coffee of his own invention, made from burnt oats, soaked in brine.

ERUCT *v.* (uh RUHKT) to belch

Although impolite in most Western cultures, *eructing* after a meal is considered a complement in some cultures.

Noxious fumes *eructed* from the top of Mount Saint Helens adumbrating the coming destruction.

ESCHATOLOGY *n.* (es kuh TAHL uh jee) doctrine or belief in the last judgment or the end of humanity

Ronald Reagan allegedly held a firm belief in the *eschatological* tenets listed in revelations. Some theorists believe his buildup of nuclear arms was in preparation for the second coming.

ESCHEW *v.* (uhs CHOO) to shun

> To *eschew* tediousness, we shall end this sentence here.
> What cannot be *eschew'd*, must be embrac'd
> —from *Merry Wives of Windsor*, by William Shakespheare

QUICK QUIZ #22

Match each word in the first column with its definition in the second column. Check your answers in the back.

1. epigone	a. imitator
2. epiphany	b. shun
3. epistemology	c. imitation
4. epistolary	d. counterbalanced
5. eponymous	e. sudden understanding
6. equipoise	f. study of knowledge
7. ersatz	g. belch
8. eruct	h. about letters
9. eschatology	i. named after
10. eschew	j. belief in the last judgement

ESURIENT *adj.* (uh SOO ree uhnt) hungry, greedy

> Unable to flee any longer, the mouse fell into the *esurient* grasp of the feral cat.

> After slipping on the ice in front of the Microsoft building, I was tracked down by a tassel of *esurient* litigators, eager to get their hands on my case.

ETHNOCENTRIC *adj.* (ETH noh sen trik) belief in the supremacy of one's race or ethnic group

> Someone who is ethnocentric habitually judges a foreign people's conduct through his own ethical system.

> Only through discarding our pervasive *ethnocentrism* will we be able to embrace the greatness present in other cultures.

> Some argue that a familiarity with a foreign tongue can make us less *ethnocentric* and more willing to accept diversity.

ETHOS *n.* (EE thaws) the character or values of a specific person, culture, movement

> Understanding the general *ethos* of the American people is all it takes to become a successful politician.

> If the *ethos* of the century is greed, than Khravis epitomized this sense, grabbing money whenever possible, often at the expense of impoverished elderly women.

> The *ethos* of science is that the simplest theory that explains the most, is considered valid.

ETIOLATED *adj.* (EET ee uh lay tuhd) to whiten or become bleached

Although you might not realize it, celery in the store would be as green as broccoli flourettes, had it not been *etiolated*.

I... left a bullet in one of his poor *etiolated* arms.
—from *Jane Eyre*, by Charlotte Brontë)

ETIOLOGY *n.* (eet ee AHL uh jee) the study of causes or origins; assignment of a cause, a cause of a disease (also aetiology)

Through *etiology*, he hoped to understand the origins of certain customs, but for the most part, they remained a mystery.

When physicians finally discovered the *etiology* of malaria, they were surprised that a mosquito bite could cause such damage.

EUDAEMONISM *n.* (yoo DEE muh niz uhm) an ethical system of values that measures and evaluates actions by their ability to produce happiness (sometimes eudemonism)

The baby-boom generation is often accused of *eudaemonism*; they will often make decisions solely on the basis of whether an action will make them happy.

EUGENICS *n.* (yoo JEN iks) the study of ways in which to improve the human race through genetic breeding.

The most obvious example of *eugenics* is the Nazi "final solution" in which Hitler and his henchmen attempted to purify the Aryan race by exterminating Jews and other undesirables.

Even the United States government advocated *eugenics* for a while, suggesting the sterilization of people with low IQs.

EURYTHMICS *n.* (yoo RITH miks) the art of performing certain types of rhythmic moving to music (also eurhythmics)

Eurythmics were originally meant to have an educational value. Professor Jacques-Dalcroze created the dancing system and coined the term.

In the early part of the century, many schools provided education in dance and *eurythmics* as part of their normal curriculum.

EXCORIATE *v.* (ek SKOH ree ayt) to abrade, to wear the skin off; to denounce scathingly

Close contact with the flame had *excoriated* the tips of my fingers.

EXCULPATE *v.* (EK skuhl payt) to free from blame, to prove to be guiltless

Having been caught in the act of stealing cookies, he found it extremely difficult to *exculpate* himself.

QUICK QUIZ #23

Match each word in the first column with its definition in the second column. Check your answers in the back.

1. esurient	a. ethnic supremacy
2. ethnocentric	b. to wear away
3. ethos	c. blanch
4. etiolated	d. greedy
5. etiology	e. study of causes
6. eudaemonism	f. acquit
7. eugenics	g. dancing
8. eurythmics	h. character of a people
9. excoriate	i. human breeding
10. exculpate	j. hedonism

EXIGUOUS *adj.* (eg ZIG yuh wuhs) scanty, meager

Exiguous differs from meager, sparse and scanty in a subtle way. While meager describes that which is small or inadequate, and scanty might describe something barely adequate, something that is *exiguous* is scanty in such a way as to compare unfavorably with anything else of its kind.

Teacher's pay in some communities is in the highest degree *exiguous*, barely enough to survive, let alone support a family.

EXTIRPATE *v.* (EKS tuhr payt) to rip up by the roots; to abolish or exterminate; to remove by surgery

Kudzu grows so quickly that the only way to contain a colony is to completely *extirpate* it.

The Christian nation held, as one of its most fundamental beliefs, that it must *extirpate* any Muslims in its midst.

One of Robespierre's goals was to *extirpate* monarchy and other regal powers from the entire world. He succeeded in France with his friend, the guillotine.

FABULIST *n.* (FAB yuh luhst) someone who invents fables; someone who tells lies

The great *fabulist*, Aesop, was a real figure, whose stories have influenced millions.

It took Martin quite a while to figure out that his host was an egregious *fabulist*.

FACTITIOUS *adj.* (fak TIH shuhs) formed unnaturally

Something that is factitious is produced in an artificial manner. To say that something came about factitiously is to imply it was somehow forced into being by human agency.

Several of the dunes in the desert are obviously *factitious*; if I were to dig for buried treasure, that's where I'd start.

Stonehenge in England is composed of enormous stones that seem to be carved by human hands but are surprisingly not *factitious*.

FARRAGO *n.* (fuh RAH goh) a medley, a mixture

This word derives from a mixture of food for cattle. It often suggests a confused mixture.

He was convinced that such a *farrago* of half-truths posed great danger.

Holmes was presented with a *farrago* of facts, and his job was to find those with relevance and solve the murder.

FEBRILE *adj.* (FEB ryel) or (FEEB ryel) feverish; *n.* febrility (fuh BRIL uhd ee)

Eating the poisoned fish put us all in a *febrile* state. We could not do enough to keep warm.

The ideas expressed in the work are so clever and so new, only a *febrile* intelligence could have written such a book.

FECKLESS *adj.* (FEK luhs) lacking strength, ineffective; irresponsible

Feck comes from "effect" and used to mean the purpose of a statement "without effect."

We knew we had little to fear from the *feckless* widow living below us, but we still acted cautiously.

Almost forty years of *feckless* negotiation in the Middle East has yet to yield lasting peace.

FERAL *adj.* (FIR uhl) or (FER uhl) wild by nature; tame animals whose descendants have become wild; like a wild animal

Eve was surprised at the *feral* hostility she encountered whenever she entered the room. Perhaps it was her new perfume "wild one."

Many aboriginal animals of Australia are being killed by gangs of *feral* cats and rabbits which are extremely efficient hunters.

FETID *adj.* (FED uhd) smelly

For giving man fire, Prometheus's punishment was to have vultures tear out his liver with their *fetid* beaks, at which point the organ would regenerate and be plucked out anew.

Recovering from her hangover, Briget had to deal not only with a headache but with the *fetid* odor of used ashtrays too.

FEY *adj.* (FAY) mad, out of one's mind; magical; otherworldly, able to see fairies

Originally fey meant doomed to die, but its current meaning derives from an excited state that was thought to precede death.

She kept cranking out enchanting *fey* novels that caused her readers to go mad.

She was not sensible like her sister, but *fey*, and was often found staring off in a dreamlike state.

QUICK QUIZ #24

Match each word in the first column with its definition in the second column. Check your answers in the back.

1. exiguous	a. mixture
2. extirpate	b. stinky
3. fabulist	c. wild
4. factitious	d. man made
5. farrago	e. destroy
6. febrile	f. ineffective
7. feckless	g. liar
8. feral	h. feverish
9. fetid	i. magical
10. fey	j. meager

FILIBUSTER *n.* (FIL uh buhs tuhr) obstructing the passing of legislation by speaking with the sole purpose of delay; one who fights in a foreign country privately; *v.* to obstruct legislation by filibuster; to take part in revolutionary activities in a foreign country

All by himself, Senator L'Gatto was able to carry on a *filibuster* that lasted 24 hours without even so much as a break for a glass of water. L'Gatto said it came from her years of practice as an auctioneer.

Colonel South was surprised to encounter another *filibuster* in his fight for Nicaraguan independence.

Much legislation never reaches a vote in the Senate, where a lone speaker can *filibuster* for hours, wearing down opposition and wasting time.

FILLIP *n.* (FIL uhp) the snap made when a finger is pressed and held against one's thumb and then suddenly released; a small stimulus (also filip) *v.* to strike with a fillip, to stimulate

The little tyke, by *fillip*, made the ketchup fly.

He judged the quality of the glass by giving it a *fillip* and counting how long the sound rang.

The war in Iraq gave a brief *fillip* to American patriotism, but people were soon grumbling about the lack of good jobs.

FLAGELLATE *v.* (FLAJ uh layt) to whip; to punish as if by whipping

The punishment in Singapore for even a minor offense is *flagellation*.

He tied himself to his desk chair and *flagellated* himself with the daily job of writing his novel.

FLAGITIOUS *adj.* (fluh JIH shuhs) vicious, characterized by cruelty or brutality, extremely wicked; scandalous

Morton was the most *flagitious* of criminals, killing without remorse and then eating his victims.

The Chinese government continued its *flagitious* policy of destroying all aspects of Tibetan culture in what is often termed cultural genocide.

FLEER *v.* (FLIR) to smirk in contempt, to leer; *n.* a derisive look, a sneer; *adv.* fleeringly (FLIR ing lee)

After eructing, he might have apologized, but instead grinned and *fleered* in my face.

Do but encave yourself,
And mark the *fleers*, the gibes, and notable scorns,
That dwell in every region of his face
—from *Othello*, by William Shakespeare

FOP *n.* (FAHP) a dandy, coxcomb, a man overly concerned with (and usually vain about) his manners and clothes.

He knew that there was no hope for meaningful conversation at this gallery opening attended by a group of *fops* who kept admiring themselves in the full length mirror.

FRACTIOUS *adj.* (FRAK shuhs) unruly, with a tendency to make trouble; cranky

Marlene was a *fractious* baby whose screams were enough to waken the dead.

He stumbled on to the stage and prepared to address the *fractious* crowd which had been waiting for almost three hours.

FRIBBLE *v.* (FRIB buhl) to fritter away; *n.* a frivolous person; *adj.* frivolous

With ten hours to go before the next train, all we could do was *fribble* away the time by playing cards.

She watched shocked as he *fribbled* away his fortune at the casino.

Frank was a *fribble* fellow who, every day, wore new pocket handkerchiefs sticking proudly out of his vest pocket.

FROUFROU *adj.* (FROO froo) excessively fussy or showy ornamentation or dress; a rustling sound

He was ambivalent about buying the mansion, overwhelmed by the *froufrou* of Victorian architecture.

It was hard to hear the opera over the *froufrou* of the dresses and the coughing of the bored audience.

FROWARD *adj.* (FROH wuhrd) contrary, habitually disobedient

Although "contrary" and "froward" have almost the same meaning, froward suggests a more habitual contrariness. The word comes from "fro" (as in to and fro) and suggests one who is always going away from the suggested path.

Dorine could only find peace in her home, by treating her husband as a mother would treat a *froward* child. When he made a mess, she scolded him, when he was good she gave him some Pablum.

Match each word in the first column with its definition in the second column. Check your answers in the back.

1. filibuster		a. showy
2. fillip		b. cranky
3. flagellate		c. contrary
4. flagitious		d. waste time
5. fleer		e. snap
6. fop		f. obstructive speech
7. fractious		g. whip
8. fribble		h. sneer
9. froufrou		i. dandy
10. froward		j. vicious

FUGACIOUS *adj.* (fyoo GAY shuhs) evanescent, lasting only a short time

When this word is used to describe immaterial objects, it means evanescent; when it describes substances, it usually means volatile or unfixed.

In electronic town meetings, decisions are based on the most *fugacious* of elements: public opinion.

Life was hard when he had to work in the Naval Yard; it was to much work with few *fugacious* pleasures mixed in.

Compared to coal, natural gas is *fugacious*, and as such, it must be mined with care.

FULGENT *adj.* (FOOL juhnt) or (FUHL juhnt) dazzlingly bright, radiant

Blinded by the fulgent sun, we sought the shade of a sycamore tree to sip our tea.

The beauty of the *fulgent* narcissi against the dark wall was nearly overwhelming.

At last as from a Cloud his *fulgent* head
And shape Starr bright appeer'd, or brighter, clad
With what permissive glory since his fall
Was left him, or false glitter:
—from *Paradise Lost*, by John Milton

FULSOME *adj.* (FOOL suhm) offensive, especially because of excess or insincerity; unctuous

Fulsome originally meant abundant, but this meaning recently became obsolete, when people misused the word to mean offensive or insincere. This type of usage can lead to confusion. "Fulsome apologies," for example, might mean a lot of apologizing (in a good way), or it could mean so much apologizing as to be in bad taste. You would be much safer saying a "full apology."

Yusef's praise for his mother's cooking was not quite *fulsome*. Comparing her deserts to a midnight summer's dream was just on the edge of good taste.

The *fulsome* glitter from the rhinestone studs encased in Elvis's clothing stood out at the genteel gathering.

FUNGIBLE *adj.* (FUHN juh buhl) (Law) able to replace something of equal value, e.g. a quantity of grain that can replace the same amount; interchangeable

The ancient laws were simple, if somebody destroyed *fungible* property, he replaced it; if he destroyed property that was not *fungible*, he was required to replace it with something of comparable value.

FUSILLADE *n.* (FYOO suh layd) a rapid or simultaneous discharge of many firearms or a firing squad; by extension, a rapid outburst in quick succession

The deer valiantly attempted to escape, but was hit with a *fusillade* of buckshot and died instantly.

Only in Utah are executions still done by *fusillade*; elsewhere, states use lethal injection.

Wearing the wrong color for spring, she was hit by a *fusillade* of surprisingly vitriolic insults upon entering the room.

FUSTIAN *n.* (FUHS chuhn) a thick, twilled cloth (e.g. corduroy); pompous speech or writing; *adj.* made of such cloth; pompous

Just as the word "bombast," refers to stuffed cotton and to a stuffed-shirt type of speech, fustian fabric is puffed up beyond its normal state.

His pants were made of *fustian*, his shirt of wool, but he was shoeless in the frigid rain.

The speech was pure political *fustian*; in two hours of "yours truly" and "humble service," not one word of substance was uttered.

The professor had seen turgid writing before, but Shmendrick's *fustian* style was unbearable.

FUSTY *adj.* (FUHS tee) musty, mildewy; old fashioned, antiquated

It had been ten years since someone had entered her *fusty* old attic. Who would have thought she would find the grisly remains of the family dog.

She knew it would be unpleasant to stay at an inn that was nasty, dusty, and *fusty*, but what choice did she have? She could drive no longer.

He opened the door and saw at his stoop a *fusty* old gentleman in a poorly made suit.

GAD *v.* (GAD) to wander with no apparent purpose

The coxcomb, dressed in all his finery, was seen *gadding* about gossiping with every other fop in this awful seaside town.

Johnson spent the two years after college *gadding* about the world searching for adventure and love; he found neither.

A "gadfly," by the way, is either a fly that bites livestock or a purposely annoying person whose persistent criticism drives his victims to distraction.

Upton Sinclair was a noted *gadfly* to industrialists, writing books that forced government regulation.

GALLIVANT v. (GAL uh vant) to bop about happily, esp. with members of the opposite sex (also galavant and gallavant)

Instead of studying for his finals, he spent the entire night *gallivanting* with the dean's daughter.

GAMIN n. (GAM uhn) a street urchin (gamin is male, gamine female); *adj.* like a gamin(e)

A "gamine" can also mean a slim mischievous girl with an elfish charm.

He knew it was time to leave when out of the corner of his eye he saw a *gamin* tossing stones at his car.

The beggar was a sixty-year-old man with a tough *gamin* face who often scared people into giving him money.

Dressed in outlandish outfits, high-priced supermodels sashayed down the aisles, their figures shapely *gamine* lines.

QUICK QUIZ #26

Match each word in the first column with its definition in the second column. Check your answers in the back.

1. fugacious	a. offensively excessive
2. fulgent	b. flirt
3. fulsome	c. burst
4. fungible	d. brilliant
5. fusillade	e. replaceable
6. fustian	f. pompous language
7. fusty	g. street kid
8. gad	h. wander
9. gallivant	i. passing
10. gamin	j. musty

GARROTE n. (guh RAHT) or (ga ROH) a Spanish method of execution in which an iron collar is tightened around the condemned person's neck; such an iron collar; strangulation (to rob); a cord used to strangle; v. (also garrotte) to use a garrotte for execution; to commit robbery by strangling from behind

Juan was lucky enough to avoid the *garrote* when caught stealing the queen's bloomers, but he was still forced to spend an evening on the rack.

He spent a week perfecting his *garrote*, made with piano wire and two wooden handles, and now, the day before his assignment, he could not keep his hands off it.

GEMEINSCHAFT n. (ge MYEN shahft) a group with similar tastes or a strong sense of identity

A sociological construct, this word describes a "natural" group, one in which the members have affection, kinship, or are part of the same community. It is usually contrasted with "gesellschaft" (ge ZEL shahft) which is a group with similar goals that is thrown together in some factitious way. A family group would be a gemeinschaft while a corporate office would most likely be a gesellschaft.

Both *gemeinschaft* and gesellschaft represent positive types of social relationships, that is, they represent people working together.

GEMÜTLICH *v.* agreeable

The decorator had added a pale green sofa which somehow gave the room a more *gemütlich* quality.

He was pleased to see such a plump *gemütlich* German lady waiting at the door to his new villa.

GENUFLECT *v.* (JEN yuh flekt) to bend one's knees or touch a knee to the ground in worship; to grovel

She entered the chapel, unsure of how to proceed, and *genuflected* three times before taking her seat.

When all other avenues of negotiation had failed, his only recourse was to *genuflect* before the C.E.O. and hope that her sense of mercy would get him his job back.

GERRYMANDER *v.* (JEH ree man duhr) to set up lines for political districts so that the party in power is more likely to win an election; *n.* the act of gerrymandering; a gerrymandered district

This word is derived from a 19th century political event. Governor Elbridge Gerry (GEH ree) of Massachusetts had signed a bill in 1811 that set up representative districts that favored the Democrats over the Federalists, despite that fact that the Federalists won nearly two thirds of the votes cast in the previous election. When Gilbert Stuart (the painter who did the portrait of George Washington used on the dollar bill), then working at the Boston Sentinel, saw the map from the bill, he sketched a few lines on top of one of the districts and called it a salamander. The editor of the paper allegedly replied: "Salamander? Call it a Gerrymander!" and subsequently, the term became a rallying cry for Federalists in Massachusetts.

The democratic congressional committee in charge of redistricting was able to *gerrymander* the entire state of New York to ensure another democratic victory.

GESTALT *n.* (geh SHTAHLT) a group or configuration whose individual parts cannot stand alone, nor can they be understood as simply the summation of the elements

This word describes a structure whose parts cannot stand alone; for example, a melody is *gestalt* because the notes that make it up if looked at individually do not describe it. The word is also used in describing Gestalt psychology, a theory that believes that it is impossible to understand any psychological or physiological phenomenon as a simple summation of sense perceptions.

Dr. Cramer was a *Gestalt* psychologist, and as such, looked at the whole picture of her patients' diseases.

Although the critic aptly described the usage of language in Marcel's new poem, he misunderstood the *gestalt* of the work.

GEVALT *interj.* (guh VUHLT (tktk check pronunciation)) (Yiddish) a strong exclamation for help or out of fear; desperate expression of protest.

This word today is most often heard in the expression "Oy gevalt", which describes intense dismay.

"*Gevalt!*" cried Solly, clutching his dome after being hit with a stray golf ball. Mr. Hovitz, the golfer who had teed off, hurried up with apologies.
—from *Joys of Yinglish*, Leo Rosten

GIRD *v.* (GUHRD) to encircle as with a belt; to prepare for action (usually gird up)

She *girded* herself with a multicolored apron and prepared to cook another gourmet meal for a thankless clan of philistines.

They dressed and then *girded* up to face the chaos of the city streets.

The tortures inflicted on the prisoner only served to *gird* his soul with new endurance.

GLABROUS *adj.* (GLAY bruhs) without hair; smooth

The sea onion, a remarkably ugly plant, with an etiolated, *glabrous* bulbous base, is remarkably popular among plant collectors.

The makeup artist, used to dealing with teenagers, was unable to compensate for Xerses' *glabrous* pate, which shone like a pool cue in the television lights.

GLOZE *v.* (GLOHZ) to palliate; to minimize; to gloss (over)

In attempting to be thorough in his analysis of voting patterns, the researcher *glozed* over nothing.

Although the Bush presidency would have preferred its history *glozed* over, investigative reporters would not let the Iran Contra scandal disappear.

QUICK QUIZ #27

Match each word in the first column with its definition in the second column. Check your answers in the back.

1. garrote	a. redistrict unfairly
2. gemeinschaft	b. SH*T!
3. gemütlich	c. encircle
4. genuflect	d. group
5. gerrymander	e. minimize
6. gestalt	f. curtsy
7. gevalt	g. bald
8. gird	h. strangle
9. glabrous	i. wholeness
10. gloze	j. agreeable

GOBBET *n.* (GAH buht) a chunk or piece, esp. of raw flesh; a lump, or morsel; a mouthful

The fin of the shark has no culinary value, so we choped it into *gobbets* and fed it to the dogs.

The article, although long and turgid, did contain several *gobbets* of useful information.

GONIF *n*. (GAH nuhf) a thief, an untrustworthy person, a mischievous child, an ingenious person.

"You bought a car from that *gonif*," said my mother, "you deserve all that you get."

GOOGOL *n*. (GOO gawl) ten to the 100th power

"Googol " was invented by Dr. Edward Kasner's nine-year-old nephew when the boy was asked to name a really big number. He also came up with the name "googolplex" which indicates one followed by a googol of zeroes.

The young actor knew that the chances of success were one in a *googol*, but she pressed on in hopes of becoming a star.

GRAND GUIGNOL *n*. (grahn geen YAWL) a type of drama that emphasizes the macabre

Literally meaning "great punch," Grand Guignol is the name of a theater in Paris that specialized in macabre plays. It now has the more general meaning of a drama that is horrifying or macabre.

A dark and foreboding film, *Death by Laughing* is the perfect example of *Grand Guignol*. It features over two hours of torture, violence, and demons.

GRIG *n*. (GRIG) a lively person

Learning of her daughter's engagement, she became merry as a *grig*, jumping about and singing to herself.

As a young *grig*, I led a carefree life, but was not too hopeful about my future.

GROAK *n*. (GROHK) a person or animal that hangs around watching hopefully for some food

This exceedingly rare word seems so perfect for describing a class of people who have been aptly characterized in a number of sit-coms: the person who always shows up, ready to eat, right around dinner time.

Mrs. Johnson's *groak* of a son-in-law would show up, unannounced, at exactly 6:00 with fork in hand.

The hyenas stood *groak*-like waiting for the lions to finish their meal.

GYMNOSOPHIST *n*. (jim NAH suh fist) a member of an ancient Hindu sect that wore no cloths and meditated a lot

n. gymnosophy (jim NAH suh fee)

According to ancient reports, while the gymnosophists eschewed clothing, they were very concerned with their beards, which they felt had a mystical quality.

Many of the Greeks traveled East in search of the secrets of the *gymnosophists*, but none could master the arcane cult.

HABEAS CORPUS *n.* (HAY bee uh SKAWR puhs) a writ or order causing a prisoner to come before a judge to determine the legality of his sentence

Recently, the supreme court has been restricting the writ of *habeas corpus,* despite the fact that it is expressly given in the Constitution.

"The privilege of the writ of *habeas corpus* shall not be suspended, unless when in cases of rebellion or invasion, the public safety may require it."
—from the U.S. Constitution

Even though he was imprisoned illegally, he was in a country that disallowed the writ of *habeas corpus,* and as such he was doomed to die in jail.

HAGIOGRAPHY *n.* (HA gee uh gra fee) or (HA gee uh gra fee) a biography of saints; a biography that idealizes or worships its subject

A *hagiographer* by trade, he did not consider himself a true historian.

Samuel's biography of Hank Aaron certainly bordered on *hagiography;* not one word or criticism was even suggested.

HALITOSIS *n.* (hal uh TOH suhs) bad breath

He had successfully wooed the most beautiful girl in school when his darned *halitosis* got in his way. As he got near enough to kiss her, she turned away and retched.

The room had the fetid smell of a hundred people with *halitosis.*

QUICK QUIZ #28

Match each word in the first column with its definition in the second column. Check your answers in the back.

1. gobbet		a.	food watcher
2. gonif		b.	order giving prisoner second chance
3. googol		c.	nude meditators
4. Grand Guignol		d.	lively person
5. grig		e.	macabre drama
6. groak		f.	huge number
7. gymnosophist		g.	bad breath
8. habeas corpus		h.	biography of saints
9. hagiography		i.	chunk
10. halitosis		j.	thief

HANDSEL *n.* (Han suhl) a gift given to wish good luck for a new year or a new enterprise; the first money received by a business or enterprise usually signifying good luck (also hansel)

In England among the aristocracy, it is common practice to give a *handsel* to each servant at the start of the new year.

Every day, after making the first sale, he waited until the customer had left and kissed the *handsel* for good luck.

HEGIRA n. (heh JYE ruh) or (heh JUH ruh) an escape to avoid danger or to reach a highly desirable location

Hegira with a capital H refers to the flight of Mohammed from Mecca to Medina in 622, and is used to refer to the Islamic era. (also hejira)

After the hurricane, the people went on long *hegiras* searching for arable land.

When the temperature approaches 90 degrees, much of Manhattan's Upper East Side plans a *hegira* to the relative cool of Long Island beaches.

The antisemitism in Europe preceding the Holocaust caused a *hegira* of Jewish intellectuals who pursued their careers in the United States.

HERMENEUTICS n. (huhr muh NYOOD iks) the science of interpretation (esp. spiritual texts) (the word can be written with either a singular or plural verb)

Clever use of *hermeneutics* can prove a weapon in arguing any ecclesiastical point. Such study of interpretations is foregone by certain religions that pursue a personal relationship with the bible.

HETERODOX adj. (HED uhr uh dahks) iconoclastic, not in agreement with accepted beliefs, unorthodox

Boregaurd the cat held some *heterodox* opinions about the best way to build a mouse trap.

Nailing Martin Luther's *heterodox* theses upon the post ended five hundred years of domination by Roman Catholic doctrine.

Nixon, whose presidency was undone by the Watergate scandal, had *heterodox* views on the ethics of campaigning.

HEURISTIC adj. (hyoor RIST ik) or (HYOOR rist ik) of or related to speculation as a method of learning, serving to discover; (education) related to a type of learning in which a student is encouraged to discover rather than be taught; (computers) a method of programming in which the program makes decisions in stages, deciding at each stage where to proceed; n. a heuristic process; heuristics, the study of the heuristic process

Making a *heuristic* assumption about the speed of light, Einstein was able to uncover vast secrets of the universe.

Although vague, his assumption proved *heuristic*, enabling him to gain a great deal of understanding from a premise that was, at best, dubious.

Although it takes more effort, the *heuristic* method of education has enabled students to comprehend concepts that before they had only learned by rote.

HIRSUTE adj. (HER soot) covered with hair

At first, the *hirsute* man on the subway seemed dangerous, but when he smiled he looked like Santa Claus.

He entered the bathroom appearing wild and *hirsute*, but left it a clean cut well scrubbed individual.

Jacob fooled old, blind Isaac by wrapping himself in animal fur to impersonate his *hirsute* brother, and in this way was able to steal his father's blessing.

HOBSON'S CHOICE *n.* (hahb suhnz CHOIS) a choice where one must take what is offered or must take nothing at all

The phrase is derived from Hobson who rented horses in Cambridge England. Although a customer saw a stable full of horses, and so apparently, had a choice among many, he was forced to take the horse which was standing next to the stable door.

While reading the long list of specials on the menu, David was suddenly faced with a *Hobson's Choice*; the waiter informed him that meatloaf was the only special still available.

HOI POLLOI *n.* (HOI puh LOI) the masses

Although hoi polloi literally means "the many," it is often used in English preceded by the definite article: "the." Although this is redundant it has become fairly accepted. Recently, the word has been misused to mean the elite.

The cultural elite attending Harvard spend a good deal of their time disdaining the *hoi polloi* while living well spending their parents' hard earned money.

One of the arguments against Public Television is that *hoi polloi* don't watch it, and the cultural elite can afford to pay for their own TV.

HOMOLOGATE *v.* (hoh MAHL uh gayt) to confirm officially

The President signed the treaty with Japan, and the senate afterwards *homologated* the agreement.

By failing to appeal, he had basically *homologated* the court's judgment of his guilt.

HOMUNCULUS *n.* (hoh MUHN kyuh luhs) a dwarf, a small human; a tiny human beleived by early biologists to live in a sperm cell

Before scientists knew better, they believed that a *homunculus* lived in every sperm cell, and gradually grew into a human being.

Standing before us in the doctor's office was a *homunculus* of only about four feet tall.

QUICK QUIZ #29

Match each word in the first column with its definition in the second column. Check your answers in the back.

1. handsel	a. confirm
2. hegira	b. a limited choice
3. hermeneutics	c. hairy
4. heterodox	d. science of interpretation
5. heuristic	e. iconoclastic
6. hirsute	f. speculative
7. hobson's choice	g. the masses
8. hoi polloi	h. good luck gift
9. homologate	i. escape
10. homunculous	j. dwarf

HOOTENANNY *n.* (HOOT uhn an nee) a "thingamajig"; an informal jam session of singers with participation from the audience (also hootnanny and hootananny)

Hootenanny, like thingamajig, is a word that you can use to describe that whosee on the watchamacallit, especially if it's a gizmo whose standard name is unfamiliar; it also describes a folk-music jam session.

I've been diddling with that *hootenanny* on the left side of the circuit breaker, but I can't get the lights to go on.

It's not enough to simply attend a *hootenanny*, one must be prepared to pull out one's ukulele and play along.

HORTATIVE *adj.* (HOR tay tiv) giving advice; encouraging, inciting

The dean's commencement speech was replete with *hortative* digressions that were completely ignored by the new alumnae.

HOYDEN *n.* (HOI duhn) a rude girl; a tomboy; *adj.* like a hoyden

Jomel was anything but a *hoyden*; elegant and sophisticated, she impressed all who met her.

Maxine had taken up with a group of country *hoydens*, who took her to hootenannies and taught her to slap her thigh with the appropriate gusto.

HUGGER-MUGGER *n.* (HUHG guhr muhg uhr) confusion, jumble; secrecy (also huggermugger) *adj.* confused; secret

Although years ago a child conceived out of wedlock was a source of shame and was kept secret from all but one's closest friends, today it is treated without any *hugger-mugger* at all.

The absent-minded professor, sat in a *hugger-mugger* of papers, frantically searching for the one that would allow him to pick up his dry cleaning.

Ricardo awoke in a friendly, if *hugger-mugger*, cottage, watched by two of the most gemütlich old women he had ever had the pleasure to meet.

HULLABALOO *n.* (HUL luh buh loo) uproar, great noise or excitement; excited confusion (also hullaballoo and hellaballoo)

Lexicographers aren't sure about the derivation of this word; some assume that it is a combination of hallo (like today's "yo!") and a Scottish word baloo, an interjection used like "hush" to quiet children. Others feel that it is a repetition of the word hallo.

He screamed above the *hullabaloo* of the New Year's Eve party, trying, and failing, to get his date's attention.

An argument over who was the top Barbara Streisand imitator created such a *hullabaloo* that the theater was shut down by the LAPD.

HUSTINGS *n.* (HUHS tins) or (HUHS teens) any place where election campaign speeches are made; an act of political campaigning

This year's *hustings* provided much more controversy than the usual odd-year election.

HYPOMANIA *n.* (HYE poh may nee uh) a mild mania

This word describes a mild feeling of elation and well-being that is part of the manic-depressive cycle. Some have theorized that many creative people feel most productive when they are in a hypomanic state. The word comes from a combination of hypo (under or less than) and mania (meaning mental hyperactivity) which in turn comes from the Greek word mainesthai (to be mad).

Although clearly not psychotic, Crazy Benny's *hypomania* caused his friends concern. Lately, he had been sleeping little and spending almost all of his time studying.

IDEATE *v.* (EYE dee ayt) or (eye DEE ayt) to form an idea, to conceive

Choreographer Mary *ideated* many steps that were physically impossible to perform.

The horrors of war, while real enough, are impossible for a civilian to *ideate* without some actual experience in combat.

(*Ideate* is a common crossword puzzle word.)

IGNEOUS *adj.* (IG nee uhs) relating to fire; formed from a molten state (geology); related to such rock

Although at first glance he thought it lifeless, Leslie was surprised to find that many plants thrived in the desert's *igneous* atmosphere.

The geologists, upon seeing basalt and other *igneous* rocks, realized that they were looking at the detritus of an ancient volcano.

IMAGO *n.* (uh MAY goh) or (uh MAH goh) an adult stage of an insect; (psychology) an ideal image of a parent or other person formed in childhood but remaining unconsciously in adulthood

Although the *imago* of the tent moth isn't harmful, its larvae eat the budding leaves of apple trees.

Whenever college freshman Johnny got a call from his mother, he would unconsciously respond to the mother-*imago* by sticking his thumb in his mouth.

Quick Quiz #30

Match each word in the first column with its definition in the second column. Check your answers in the back of the book.

1. hootenanny	a. encouraging
2. hortative	b. uproar
3. hoyden	c. imagine
4. hugger-mugger	d. jam session
5. hullabaloo	e. like fire
6. hustings	f. feeling of elation
7. hypomania	g. tomboy
8. ideate	h. a mature insect
9. igneous	i. place for speeches
10. imago	j. confusion

IMBROGLIO *n.* (uhm BROHL yoh) a difficult situation; a complicated disagreement; a confused mass (also embroglio—em BROHL yoh)

On the top of his desk lay an *imbroglio* of used envelopes and dirty laundry.

Once he reached the age of 90, his affairs had degenerated into a hopeless *imbroglio* that even his accountant granddaughter could not untangle.

IMMOLATE *v.* (IM uh layt) to kill as a sacrificial victim; to commit suicide by fire; to destroy

The indigenous people of the island attempted to *immolate* Fay Wray to appease Kong, but the monster took a liking to her and protected her from the twin evils of dinosaurs and the press.

In a vivid statement of protest, several anti-war fanatics *immolated* themselves in front of the television cameras.

IMMURE *v.* (im MYOOR) to enclose as if within a wall; to entomb into a wall

The research team, *immured* in an isolated outpost, was ill-prepared to defend itself from such a virulent disease.

One of the Egyptians' most evil acts was the *immurement* of babies within the bricks used to build the pyramids.

IMPRECATE *v.* (IM pruh kayt) to curse

After losing the case, she *imprecated* a thousand curses on the so-called justice system.

Whenever his mother entered the room, his fiancée could be heard muttering vile *imprecations* under her breath.

IN SITU *adv.* or *adj.* (in SYE too) or (in SEE too) in its original position

Surgeons today are able to watch organs functioning *in situ* to better understand any ailments.

The new library was constructed almost entirely of *in-situ* stones taken from its three-acre grounds.

INCHOATE *adj.* (in KOH uht) or (IN kuh wayt) in an early stage; imperfectly formed

Although he had spent years developing his theory, the scientific community found it *inchoate* and sent him back into the laboratory.

Carlos had only a vague, *inchoate* sense of what to expect from this first meeting with his prospective employers.

INCUNABULA *n.* (uhn KYOO nuh byuh luh) a book from before the invention of the printing press (1501); anything in its infancy

This word comes from the Latin incu-na-bula meaning swaddling clothes and can refer to anything in its earliest stage of development.

The Beatles were certain that they had stumbled upon the *incunabula* of a revolution.

In an antiquated fusty antique shop, a record collector bought for 25¢ some of the rarest *incunabula* of the disco era.

INDETERMINISM n. (in duh TUHR muh niz uhm) unpredictability; the philosophical theory that not everything is predetermined

An *indeterminist* believes in free will, in the ability of humans to control their actions and the results of those actions. Such a belief implies that personal moral responsibility cannot be avoided.

The Heisenberg *indeterminism* principle states that one cannot know with certainty both the position and direction of an electron; its location is unpredictable.

INTEGUMENT n. (in TEG yuh muhnt) an envelope, that which covers something

Madonna's book, filled with nude pictures, was covered with an opaque *integument* to discourage bookstore browsing.

INTERDICT v. (IN tuhr dikt) or (IN ter dyte) to prohibit, to forbid; to stop enemy movement by destroying supply lines

This word, when used to mean forbid or prohibit, usually implies a formal temporary prohibition which might have salutary benefits.

The airline *interdicted* the use of tobacco on any flight.

In 18th century America, women were *interdicted* many of the privileges taken for granted by men.

After the Islamic revolution in Iran, the Ayatollah *interdicted* all foreign commerce, inexorably sending the country into a recession.

QUICK QUIZ #31

Match each word in the first column with its definition in the second column. *Check your answers in the back of the book.*

1. imbroglio	a. envelope
2. immolate	b. doctrine of free will
3. immure	c. curse
4. imprecate	d. ancient book
5. in situ	e. prohibit
6. inchoate	f. in place
7. incunabula	g. sacrifice
8. indeterminism	h. intricate situation
9. integument	i. entomb
10. interdict	j. incipient

INTERREGNUM n. (in tuhr REG nuhm) the period between the end of one sovereign's reign and the beginning of another's; a period when government has stopped temporarily

In a hereditary kingdom, when there is instability, or when a sovereign dies with a heir not yet old enough to assume power, an *interregnum* can result.

The early years of the war between England and France gave the fledgling colonies an *interregnum* from British rule.

ITERANT *adj.* (IT uhr uhnt) repeating

This word is from the same root as reiterate.

The canyon shook with the *iterant* echoes of my true love's voice. She had just stepped on a scorpion.

It didn't seem to matter how many times Manny *iterated* his complaint, the post office refused to deliver his mail.

JACTITATION *n.* (JAK tuh tay shun) a false boasting or claim, esp. one that hurts others; a twitching of the body or its parts

This word today refers to a slanderous boasting, but was used especially to refer to *jactitation* of marriage, an actionable offense where someone claims a marriage that does not exist. The wounded party would file a suit of *jactitation* of marriage, which if successful, would force the offender to cease his or her false boasting.

Soap star Brenda Lee was hurt by Boris's lewd *jactitations* of their lustful affair, but her reputation was further damaged by convicted killer Dacy's jactitations of marriage.

Although Borinium's usefulness as a sedative in extreme situations is easily demonstrated, it does cause *jactitation* of the lower extremities.

JAPE *v.* (JAYP) to joke, to quip; to make fun of *n.* a joke, something meant to amuse

Because this word used to mean to have sex, it was considered obscene and was obsolete from the 16th to the early 19th century, when most people stopped using it. But 19th century writers rediscovered it and the word, in less prurient sense anyway, has come to us today.

Bigelow was just one of those kids who everyone *japed* at; no matter where he went, someone was filliping his ear, or smacking his neck. No wonder he started working for the IRS.

Upon imparting a merry *jape*, the clown exited with the ringing of children's laughter still in his ears.

JEJUNE *adj.* (juh JOON) or (jee JOON) dull; lacking in nutrition; childish

Lexicographers theorize that the third meaning, childish, comes from a mistaken assumption that the word is somehow related to the word juvenile.

Trying to impress her date, Carol sat for hours watching a *jejune* and platitudinous documentary on the lives of dung beetles: "Who Does the Doo?"

After such a thrilling adventure, it was hard to go back to the *jejune* and sterile computer manual, so Mishima surfed the net instead.

Radical Karl wondered how anyone could be so *jejune* as to believe the claim that cuts in social services would actually help the poor.

JUGGERNAUT *n.* (JUHG uhr nawt) or (JUHG uhr nahl) a massive unstoppable object that crushes anything in its path

This word comes from a Hindi word describing Jagannath, the eighth avatar of Vishnu, whose image was placed upon an enormous car and dragged through the streets. Some Westerners thought that believers who were especially fond of Vishnu would throw themselves under its wheels. Today, the word means a force that cannot be stopped and destroys all that gets in its way.

Although signing such a little slip of paper seemed an inauspicious act, it unleashed the *juggernaut* of war that would continue long after the signer had been assassinated.

His failure to successfully make Road-Runner soup placed the coyote in the path of the formidable *juggernaut* of an Acme steamroller, paving Route 66.

KIBITZ *v.* (KI buhts) to give unasked-for advice, esp. in a card game.

This Yiddish word comes from the German name for a bird Kiebitz (lapwing) which was noisy and inquisitive.

The only way to play poker at Morry's was to keep your cards hidden so that the *kibitzers* couldn't criticize your play.

KUDOS *n.* (KOO dohs) or (KYOO dahs) acclaim, praise

Kudos is singular; kudo is not a word.

For stopping the mugger from taking his wallet, Maurice received the *kudos* of his girl friend.

While a terrible lawyer is more often than not given a good deal of respect, an excellent plumber gets no *kudos*, no matter how skilled she might be.

KVETCH *n.* (KVETCH) one who complains a lot *v.* to complain

Kvetch, from Yiddish, has a meaning similar to two other Yiddish words, whose distinction, if understood, allows a writer to use scalpel-like language to describe different types of complaints. To *kvitch* is to give a little scream, perhaps out of happiness; to *kvetch* is to whine in a negative way; to *krechtz* is to moan in utter pain.

She couldn't believe that she was again listening to her brother *kvetch* about his awful job. "Why doesn't he quit already?" she wondered.

LABILE *adj.* (LAY bil) or (LAY byel) adaptable, ready to change *n.* lability (luh BIL uhd ee)

Johnson was so emotionally *labile*, that he would go from happy to sad at the same rate that a touch of a button on a remote control can change a channel.

A good actor should have a *labile* face that projects varied emotional states.

Quick Quiz #32

Match each word in the first column with its definition in the second column. Check your answers in the back of the book.

1. interregnum	a. praise
2. iterant	b. false boasting
3. jactitation	c. joke
4. jape	d. to complain
5. jejune	e. crushing vehicle
6. juggernaut	f. give advice unasked
7. kibitz	g. a break
8. kudos	h. adapatable
9. kvetch	i. dry
10. labile	j. repeating

LACHRYMOSE *adj.* (LAK ruh mohs) tearful, weepy; causing tears *adv.* lachrymosely (LAK ruh mohs lee) *n.* lachrymosity (lak ruh MAHS uhd ee)

To anyone with half a brain, Bimbata's obsession with *lachrymose* doggerel would have seemed a problem, but his fiancée felt it was normal and only became alarmed when she would find him sitting alone crying into his beer.

After being subjected to such a *lachrymose* eulogy, the mourners felt deserving of the glorious repast spread in front of them.

LACUNA *n.* (luh KOO nuh) blank space, missing part

The lawyer woke up with a start, recognizing a *lacuna* in the prosecutor's case big enough to drive a truck through.

Through clever detective work, gumshoe Doreen was able to piece together the meaning of the scrap of paper, filling up the myriad *lacunae* through educated guesses from the context.

LAPIDARY *n.* (LA puh de ree) one who cuts precious stones, a dealer in precious stones *adj.* relating to precious stones; like stone in being precise or finely defined

She just happened to look down at the right time to see a diamond the size of a strawberry between the sidewalk cracks; she had a *lapidary* set it and told everyone that she was engaged to the city.

The tall, dark, and handsome stranger had a face with *lapidary* features that drove Shannah to distraction.

The editor was unable to cut even a word from the author's *lapidary* prose.

LARIAT *n.* (LA ree uht) or (LE ree uht) a Mexican lasso

This word comes from the Spanish la reata meaning lasso. Riata (REE at uh) is also used in English to describe a *lariat*.

The cowboy threw his *lariat* around the nearest cow in an effort to stop a stampede.

LASSITUDE *n.* (LAS uh tood) a state of lethargy, weariness or listlessness

The febrile excitement of the hunt was replaced by the regretful *lassitude* caused by a failure to murder any animals for dinner.

At first her hope for release was ever-present, but eventually the prisoner settled into a morbid *lassitude*.

Had it not been for all the turkey he ate and the free-flowing wine, he might not have surrendered to an overwhelming *lassitude*, a desire to lie on the couch and watch those mind-numbing bowl games.

LEBENSRAUM *n.* (LAY benz ra oom) living space

This word, used by the Nazis to justify their insatiable desire for land, was coined by a Swedish scientist and appropriated by Karl Haushofer, a German geographer, to give a scientific rational for Germany's actions before and during World War II. In a 1942 speech, FDR deftly made use of a translation of the phrase to incite American patriotism: "The world is too small to provide adequate 'living space' for both Hitler and God." The word still has somewhat negative connotations, but is still used to describe necessary space for living.

Hitler became convinced that Poland was not sufficient for German *Lebensraum*, that the Germans would need all of Russia to survive as a nation.

LEGERDEMAIN *n.* (le juhr duh MAYN) or (LE juhr duh mayn) manual dexterity in juggling, etc.; any deception or trickery

This word comes from the French phrase "léger de main" meaning literally "light of hand," but now is used also to refer figuratively to any type of deceptive trickery.

The *legerdemain* of Murphy the Magician astonished the toddlers whose peals of laughter could bring joy to even the most heartless curmudgeon.

Through an ingeniously clever bit of diplomatic *legerdemain*, Jefferson was able to purchase the entire territory of Louisiana for mere pennies.

LEITMOTIF *n.* (lyet moh TEEF) or (LYET moh teef) (music) a repeating theme associated with a particular character (in Wagnerian opera); a dominant and recurring theme (also *leitmotiv*)

In a Wagnerian opera, a musical theme is usually assigned to specific characters, elements or situations, and when the idea or person is referred to or comes on stage, a specific *leitmotif* is played. The word is also used in a more general sense to describe any recurring theme.

Violence and murder have become the *leitmotif* of Quenel Tarantula's recent films, but unlike other violent films, his oeuvre seems not to glorify violence but to use it as a textural tool in creating an overall artistic effect.

An almost ludicrous desire to halt the spread of communism provided the *leitmotif* of U.S. foreign policy in the fifties.

LIBATION *n.* (lye BAY shun) pouring a liquid for a religious ritual; such a liquid; (informal) an intoxicating beverage; drinking such a beverage

The priest followed the prayer by performing the *libation*, pouring drops of wine onto the ground.

After striking oil in his backyard, Roger spilled a gallon or so on the ground as a *libation* to the Earth.

No matter how much she had drunk during the night, she would consume a final *libation* at her favorite bar-stool before she went home.

LIBIDINOUS *adj.* (lih BID uh nuhs) lustful; lascivious *n.* libido (li BEE doh)

Libidinous and *libido* are both from the Latin libido meaning desire or lust. *Libidinous*, however, has been an English word for at least five hundred years, while *libido* has only entered English via twentieth century psychoanalysis. *Libido* is the psychic energy usually associated with lust.

After forty years of an abstemious lifestyle, they began to participate in *libidinous* orgies that made Caligula look tame by comparison.

Many psychoanalysts assume that our sexual *libido* is thwarted by the constraints of modern society.

Many of her licentious habits could be traced to an excess of *libido*.

QUICK QUIZ #33

Match each word in the first column with its definition in the second column. Check your answers in the back of the book.

1. lachrymose	a. theme
2. lacuna	b. missing part
3. lapidary	c. a ritualistic drink
4. lariat	d. cutter of gems
5. lassitude	e. manual dexterity
6. lebensraum	f. lasso
7. legerdemain	g. weeping
8. leitmotif	h. lascivious
9. libation	i. living space
10. libidinous	j. lethargy

LICKSPITTLE *n.* (LIK spi tuhl) a toady, sycophant

It was not surprising that such a coterie of *lickspittles* would approve of the King's new suit. Any honest person would have told him that purple stripes do not go with yellow and green plaid.

Juanita's *lickspittle* humility went beyond what could be considered good taste.

LITHE *adj.* (LYTH) supple; graceful

Lithe, lithesome, and *lissome* all suggest suppleness, but subtle differences do exist in the use of the words. *Lithe* suggests nimble gracefulness, while *lithesome* may suggest an agile vigor, and *lissome* suggests a feminine grace or suppleness.

It was indeed a pleasure to watch the *lithe* young mechanic scurry underneath the car. Too bad he couldn't fix the engine.

LUBRICIOUS *adj.* (loo BRI shus) slippery; marked by instability, elusive; lewd; sexually stimulating (also lubricous (LOO bruh kuhs))

The spilled grease from the fried chicken was *lubricious* enough to cause the inexperienced chef to fall head over heels into the pot.

He is too *lubricious* to be trusted with your secrets.

The *lubricious* contents of his proposal were enough to make her blush.

LUCRE *n.* (LOO kuhr) profits, money

This word is usually used in a pejorative sense. Although *lucre* had a negative connotation even in Latin, it became shameful when William Tyndale used "filthy lucre" to refer to *aiskhron kerdos,* or "shameful gain" in his translation of the Bible. This use stuck, and the word cannot be used without some hint of evil.

Some have suggested that medicine should be a profession of honor and not of *lucre.*

LUFTMENSCH *n.* (LOOFT mench) a dreamer; a person who is impractical (also *luftmensh*)

This Yiddish word, which comes from the German luft meaning air and mensh meaning man, refers to a dreamer. As Sholem Aleicham said, "The *luftmensch* lives on hope—and hope is a liar." (p. 325 ROSTEN)

Her father, *luftmensch* extraordinare, aspired to over twenty professions but had yet to make a living out of any of them.

We have moved from an agrarian economy to a manufacturing one to a country of *luftmenschen* who buy and sell air.

MACERATE *v.* (MAS uh rayt) to make or become soft by soaking; to cause to waste away (usually be starving)

After Elsie the cow eats the grass, it is *macerated* in her stomach.

The dried spices should be *macerated* before you put them in the chicken fricassée.

Gandhi sat in prison and *macerated* himself by fasting until the British relented and changed their laws.

MANQUÉ *adj.* (mahn KAY) or (MAHn kay) one that has failed to meet his or her goal.

This word usually follows the noun it modifies.

Marjory was forced to spend the entire evening in a pretentious discussion on the merits of Proust with an intellectual *manqué* who had spent the last ten years working in a grocery store.

Only two weeks after she started working for the investment bank, Cynthia was spoken of as an artist *manqué*.

MANUMIT *v.* (MAN yuh mit) to release from slavery

From the Latin manu-mittere, which literally means to send forth from one's hand, this word means to free from bondage.

By signing the Emancipation Proclamation, Lincoln *manumitted* some four million slaves.

Prior to the Civil War, over twenty societies for the *manumission* of slaves existed in Boston alone.

MARPLOT *n.* (MAHR plaht) a foolish meddler who causes a plot to fail

Those little *marplots* had discovered too much. They were doomed to die by the hands of some ghoulish goblin.

Doctor Doom's plans to destroy the world were ruined by an unlikely group of nitwits and *marplots*, who with no help from any caped crusaders accidentally stumbled upon his fiendish scheme.

MARTINET *n.* (mahr tin ET) or (MAHR tin et) an officer who is a strict military disciplinarian; one who is a stickler for rigid adherence to rules.

This word comes from General Jean Martinet (17th century), an officer of the French army who developed a system of drills. A *martinet* is one who expects his followers to obey every rule to the letter. Martinet, ironically, was killed in 1672 by an artillery round from his own army.

General Hacker, an infernal *martinet*, insisted that we lift our legs exactly three inches when marching in formation.

The group of dowagers were led by a certain moral *martinet* who insisted that anyone who wore green in August should be castigated.

QUICK QUIZ #34

Match each word in the first column with its definition in the second column. Check your answers in the back of the book.

1. lickspittle	a.	one who wrecks plans
2. lithe	b.	slippery
3. lubricious	c.	dreamer
4. lucre	d.	unfulfilled in reaching goals
5. luftmensch	e.	profits
6. macerate	f.	to soften
7. manqué	g.	a strict disciplinarian
8. manumit	h.	graceful
9. marplot	i.	abject bootlicker
10. martinet	j.	free from bondage

MASTICATE *v.* (MAS tih kayt) to chew, to grind with the teeth; to grind

While Miller contentedly *masticated* the last bite of his fiftieth hamburger, his friends cheered him on incredulously.

Some cows will *masticate* their food for hours, waiting patiently for it to become digestible.

MELIORISM *n.* (MEE lyuh riz uhm) a theory that holds the world can be improved with well-directed human action.

Meliorism, as coined by George Eliot, falls somewhere between optimism and pessimism. A *meliorist* believes that we have the capability to improve the world, but unlike an agathist, a *meliorist* does not believe that the world will tend towards good without human agency.

Annie's activism was grounded in a firm belief in *meliorism*; she knew that she could help create a better world.

MENISCUS *n.* (mi NIS kuhs) any crescent-shaped body; a crescent-shaped lens, the crescent-shaped upper surface of a liquid

Strong eyeglasses are usually ground in the shape of a *meniscus*; one side of the lens is concave, the other convex.

To measure a liquid in a beaker, look at the bottom of the *meniscus* to get an accurate reading.

MENSCH *n.* (MENSH) an admirable trustworthy character (also *mensh*)

A *mensch* (from Yiddish) is one, who is upright, moral, better than the rest.

It's been a long time since we've had a President who legitimately qualified as a *mensch*. Roosevelt, perhaps, but even he had some illicit affair in the back country of Georgia.

MERKIN *n.* (MUHR kin) a wig for a woman's pubic hair

Paul agonized over the question of how tell his date that she had dropped her *merkin*.

METONYMY *n.* (muh TAHN uh mee) a figure of speech in which a word is substituted for a related word with which it is associated

Metonymy refers to the use of a word that taken literally would not be correct. For example, "The ruling from Washington was that we must cut our budget." Washington is used to mean the United States government.

METTLE *n.* (MET uhl) courage; quality of temperament, character

This word used to be one of the variant spellings of metal, but it gradually took on its own separate meaning. It is a type of ingrained courage. To be *on one's mettle* is to be prepared to face any challenge.

The tortures that rained on Job were guaranteed to test the *mettle* of even the strongest man.

The tragedies that had ruined his last three years served to show the *mettle* of which he was made. He survived, and grew stronger.

MIASMA *n.* (mye AZ muh) or (mee AZ muh) a poisonous vapor that was supposed to rise out of decaying material and cause malaria; any poisonous atmosphere or influence

Before scientists determined that mosquitoes carry malaria, they believed the disease was caused by a mysterious, vaporous *miasma* that came from swamps.

The local pub was a pleasant enough space if you disregarded the *miasma* of cigarette smoke emanating from forty hands holding forty Camel Lights.

From his pen flowed a *miasma* of words that would destroy the futures of the country's young people.

MIEN *n.* (MEEN) the air or bearing of a person, one's manner or personality

Lexicographers believe that "demean" came first and that this word is a shortened version, a "back-formation" in lexicographic parlance.

His downcast *mien* was enough to send his sister into a tantrum of tears.

At the drop of a hat, he could assume the *mien* of an innocuous traveler and relieve unsuspecting tourists of their hard-earned money.

MIMETIC *adj* (mi MET ik) or (mye MET ik) imitative of the natural world in literature or art; imitative

The human capacity to learn is most clearly expressed in the *mimetic* aptitude of babies who absorb knowledge at an amazing rate.

Until ballet was invented, much dance was *mimetic*, merely imitating actions from the everyday world.

QUICK QUIZ #35

Match each word in the first column with its definition in the second column. Check your answers in the back of the book.

1. masticate
2. meliorism
3. meniscus
4. mensch
5. merkin
6. metonymy
7. mettle
8. miasma
9. mien
10. mimetic

a. imitative
b. noxious vapor
c. wig for pubic hair
d. optimism
e. bearing
f. courage
g. figure of speech
h. a good man
i. chew
j. crescent-shaped body

MINATORY *adj.* (MIN uh toh ree) menacing or threatening (also *minatorial*)

The concept of freedom from government censorship is *minatory* to the religious right.

The mobster shook a *minatory* finger at me and said that I would be better off if I did not ask for my money back.

The juggernaut of Communism rumbled *minatorily* toward the Eastern European nations.

MINGY *adj.j* (MIN jee) mean and stingy; small in quantity (informal)

Lexicographers believe that *mingy* was a combination of m[ean and st]ingy, a portmanteau word.

In addition to neglecting to give his employees any health benefits, the *mingy* boss required that the employees buy their own coffee.

MINX *n.* (MINGKS) a flirtatious young woman or girl

The coxcomb, although proud of his independence, fell in love with a *minx*, and tried to make a wife out of the saucy girl.

MISCREANT *n.* (MIS kree uhnt) an evildoer; *adj.* depraved

The gang called themselves the Hootenannies, and they were a *miscreant* lot, willing to draw a knife at the least provocation.

MODICUM *n.* (MAHD uh kuhm) or (MOHD uh kuhm) a small amount

His abstemious diet consisted of a cup of green tea, a *modicum* of toast, and a fifth of whiskey.

MOIL v. (MOYIL) to toil; to work assiduously and continuously; n. drudgery, confusion

The second shift *moiled* and toiled through the night, somehow finishing the repairs so that the city could continue to have water.

A well-designed hotel should provide a break from the *moil* of everyday life.

MOLLYCODDLE v. (MAH lee cawd duhl) to indulge, to pamper; a boy who is mollycoddle n. a wimp or weakling

This word is a combination of molly, (from Mary), used to describe an effeminate man (a milksop), and coddle.

Because he never was given any responsibility and had been spoiled rotten, King George's son was a *mollycoddle*, unable or unwilling to make hard decisions or even to defend his rights.

MOOT n. (MOOT) (law) a hypothetical case or trial used as an exercise v. to discuss, to broach adj. subject to debate; of no legal significance; of no importance, made academic

Since two of its meanings are contradictory, *moot* is known as a *contranym*. To say that a point is *moot* is to say either that it is debatable or that it is unworthy of debate. Other contranyms include *cleave*, which can mean to split or to stick like glue, and *commencement*, which means the beginning of something, or the end of a period of one's education.

Although she performed admirably at Ennui Law School's weekly *moots*, Tassella could not write to save her life and failed each time she attempted the bar.

That we should have a new method for resolving such conflicts had been *mooted* many times before, but no solution has yet to be invented.

Although they had vowed to marry, the subject had not been *mooted* before her parents, who would have surely disapproved.

How he got to be President is a *moot* point—some say it is by skill, some by luck.

MORDANT adj. (MAWR duhnt) bitingly sarcastic; incisive; sharply painful

Jean was endowed with a *mordant* wit that was more likely to cause pain than to entertain.

Lord Clindiclot's *mordant* tone was even more biting than usual. Lady Mumbler was so upset that she went crying to her room.

Harry Fieldsign's humor ranged from sight gags to *mordant* satire.

MOTILE adj. (MOHT uhl) or (MOH tyle) capable of moving, mobile

(psychology) related to mental images that are formed from body movement as opposed to visual or audile.

The fungi reproduced through the agency of *motile* spores that always found themselves a host on which to grow.

While my audile friend remembers hearing the truck smash into the baby carriage, I, a *motile* type, can feel the motion that the baby must have traveled in its long arc to the ground.

Quick Quiz #36

Match each word in the first column with its definition in the second column. Check your answers in the back of the book.

1. minatory		a. academic	
2. mingy		b. villain	
3. minx		c. able to move	
4. miscreant		d. flirt	
5. modicum		e. to pamper	
6. moil		f. a wee bit	
7. mollycoddle		g. to slave	
8. moot		h. meager	
9. mordant		i. incisive	
10. motile		j. threatening	

MOUE *n.* (MOO) a pout, usually playful

Upon hearing his greeting, the minx gave a *moue* and expected him to fall rapturously in love with her. Well, she was wrong; he ignored her flirtation and went home to his family.

In response to his wife's raised eyebrow, he made a *moue* to express that it was time for them to leave.

MOUNTEBANK *n.* (MOWN tuh bangk) a conman who sells false medicines and uses jokes or tricks to attract customers; an impostor or charlatan

A contraction of the Italian "monta in banco" (mount on bench), a *mountebank* is a traveling salesman who sells nostrums through humor and chicanery.

The *mountebanks* and carpetbaggers descended on the one-horse town and sold the populace medicines that caused more harm than good.

If one wants an answer that even approaches the truth, he should avoid the *mountebanks* and frauds who are our elected officials, and instead ask the janitor who cleans their toilets.

MUCKRAKE *v.* (MUHK rayk) to expose political misconduct *n.* one who exposes political misconduct

Muckrake, as you might guess, comes from a rake used to rake muck. It was lifted out of obscurity by Theodore Roosevelt, who was annoyed by all the people dredging up muck about his administration.

After years of silence, I could not resist my duty to *muckrake* the details of the recent accident at Jack Michaelson's mansion. People need to know the extent of the cover-up.

The *muckrakers* of the early twentieth century were largely responsible for many government reforms that protect the citizens. Perhaps this administration will be responsible for the devolution of all such regulations.

MUDSILL *n.* (MUHD sil) a sill of a structure that is so low as to be in the mud; members of the lowest stratum of society

The Great Society liberals of the 1960s are turning into a *mudsill* class of liberal democrats who receive no respect and are laughed at by their more middle-of-the-road compatriots.

MUGWUMP *n.* (MUH gwuhmp) a politician who acts independently or neutrally; one who can't make up his mind

Mugwump comes from Natick, a language of the Massachusetts Indians, where it meant chief or captain. Until Republican party loyalists used it to tar their brethren who had declined to support the Republican James G. Blaine in 1884 (against Grover Cleveland), the word was jocularly used to mean a head honcho or boss. It now means one who is unable to make up his mind.

Johnstone was too much of a *mugwump* to be a leader; he couldn't make a decision to save his life.

MULCT *n.* (MUHLKT) a fine; a penalty *v.* to fine; to swindle, to bleed

In the Wild West of the eighteenth century, even the most heinous crimes could be punished with a *mulct* of livestock: rape was equal to nine head of cattle, assault to two.

The square foot of slippery sidewalk in front of Bloomingdale's gave swindler Joe an opportunity to *mulct* them for seventy thousand semolians.

MUSTH *n.* (MUHST) an annual frenzied state associated with sexual activity in male elephants (sometimes *must*)

Periodically, male elephants go *musth*, which is a mad condition in which dark brown junk exudes from pores over the eyes. At this point, they are dangerous, and should be avoided.

He knew to stay away from his mother when she got into one of her moods. She was like an elephant in *musth*.

MYRMIDON *n.* (MUHR muh dahn) a follower who faithfully obeys orders without asking questions

The Myrmidons were a warlike race of people who helped Achilles in the Trojan War. Created by Jupiter from ants to replace people who had died in a plague, Myrmidons were known for their devotion to Achilles.

Gang leader Waspola crossed the street, a set of slack-gaited *myrmidons* at his heels, and threatened the quiet of the suburban neighborhood.

NABOB *n.* (NAY bahb) a ruler in India during the Mogul Empire; a wealthy person of prominence

This word reentered American English thanks to William Safire, who inserted the phrase "nattering *nabobs* of negativism " in a speech he wrote for Nixon's Vice President, Spiro Agnew. (Nattering [NAT uhr eeng] means complaining or chattering.) Unfortunately for Agnew, such skillful wordplay could not keep him from resigning in disgrace a few years later.

I was mystified by those scientific *nabobs* discussing the ins and outs of chaos theory. I guess I picked the wrong career.

NACRE *n.* (NAY kuhr) mother-of-pearl *adj.* (also nacré [nuh KRAY] iridescent, like mother-of-pearl)

The iridescence of the *nacre* stood out against the tarnished silver of her locket.

Supermodel Progresso entered the room in a sleek, *nacre* taffeta gown that caught the eyes of everyone in the room.

QUICK QUIZ #37

Match each word in the first column with its definition in the second column. Check your answers in the back of the book.

1.	moue	a.	fine
2.	mountebank	b.	nostrom hawker
3.	muckrake	c.	expose misconduct
4.	mudsill	d.	pout
5.	mugwump	e.	mother-of-pearl
6.	mulct	f.	a vacillator
7.	musth	g.	faithful follower
8.	myrmidon	h.	elephant frenzy
9.	nabob	i.	lowest stratum
10.	nacre	j.	governor

NADIR *n.* (NAY duhr) (astronomy) the point diametrically opposed to the zenith, directly below the observer; the lowest point

Warren walked into the very *nadir* of Western civilization, a bar where thought was replaced by noise, and discussions of philosophy by cacophony.

NASCENT *adj.* (NAS uhnt) or (NAYS uhnt) emerging into existence, being born

The French sovereign should have recognized the potential of the *nascent* opposition movement and crushed it before it blossomed into a full-fledged revolution.

NEBBISH *n.* (NE bish) a hapless unfortunate, a loser (also *nebbech* and *nebbich*)

A *nebbish* is the type of person who is not noticed when he enters a room.

NEFANDOUS *adj.* (ni FAN duhs) abominable, not to be spoken of

This somewhat rare word comes from the Latin ne (not) and fandus (to speak), and means unspeakable.

He looked around the holding cell wondering what *nefandous* acts the hardy looking men might have committed.

NEOTERIC *adj.* (NEE uh ter ik) or (nee uh TER ik) modern *n.* a modern writer

Douglas was all for the *neoteric* fashion of having one's girlfriend pay for dinner. He hadn't eaten out in years.

In contradistinction to the theories of our *neoteric* philosophers, Jean's belief was that life was not an existential crisis.

The *neoterics* have dismissed the terse writing style of Hemingway for a more ornate, almost turgid, approach.

NEPENTHE *n.* (ni PEN thee) a drug or something else that helps someone forget sorrow or pain

Nepenthe was mentioned in the *Odyssey* as a drug given to Helen by the Egyptians, a drug that would dissolve a person's grief. Neoteric historians believe the drug is some form of hashish or opium.

He found that only through reading scandal-plagued boilerplate put out by the worst writers could he find *nepenthe* from his harried life.

NICTATE *v.* (NIK tayt) to wink

Many animals have a *nictating* membrane that gives added protection to their eyes.

NIGGARDLY *adj.* (NI guhrd lee) stingy; meanly small *adv.* in a stingy manner

Although etymologists are not sure of the derivation of this word, they do know that it has been around since the fourteenth century and that it is not in any way related to the modern word "nigger". To be *niggardly* is to be so cheap as to begrudge giving anything to help others.

We shouldn't be *niggardly* about this. Give everyone his fair share of the profits.

Our boss not only paid us little, but he was *niggardly* with his praise, refusing to give even the best workers a kindly pat on the back.

NIGGLE *v.* (NI guhl) to be obsessed with trivialities; to quibble, to constantly find fault with

After watching meticulous Mary spend hours on the final details of the presentation, she screamed out, "Stop *niggling* at that thing, and let's just hand it in."

He *niggled* at the food, insisting that it was too hot or too salty or not the correct shade of green. But he ate it nonetheless.

NIMBUS *n.* (NIM buhs) a luminous cloud surrounding an ancient god while on earth; an atmosphere that surrounds a person or thing; a brilliant light that surrounds a holy person, god, or emperor that is used in artistic representation to denote holiness; a rain cloud

Apollo appeared to his subjects, a *nimbus* or celestial glory surrounding him.

The church spire seemed to explode out of the ground surrounded not by the *nimbus* of staid morality, but of ethereal splendor.

The young lady entered the room and was enveloped by a *nimbus* of cheap perfume and stale cigarette smoke.

QUICK QUIZ #38

Match each word in the first column with its definition in the second column. Check your answers in the back of the book.

1. nadir	a. cloud
2. nascent	b. modern
3. nebbish	c. stingy
4. nefandous	d. lowest point
5. neoteric	e. emerging
6. nepenthe	f. wimp
7. nictate	g. abominable
8. niggardly	h. wink
9. niggle	i. quibble
10. nimbus	j. remedy for grief

NIMROD *n.* (NIM rahd) a hunter

From the Bible, this word is used to describe a hunter.

The dogs scared up the foxes, and a group of young *Nimrods* on horses followed along with their guns.

NONPLUS *v.* (nahn PLUHS) to bewilder, to make incapable of speaking or doing *n.* a state of confusion

When her fiancé's father first heard of their plans, he was *nonplused*; he had given up all hope that his son would marry.

The entire audience at the movie was *nonplused* to discover that the heroine was a he.

Murphy said to the Loan Shark "I'm at a *nonplus*, I gave my last dime to that beggar."

NOSTRUM *n.* (NAHS truhm) or (NAWS truhm) a medicine, made up of secret ingredients, whose efficacy is in question, and is usually prepared by the person selling it; a panacea

This word comes from the Latin for "ours."

The conservative's *nostrum* for the ills of society has always been to build more prisons and to take food away from the mouths of starving children.

NUGATORY *adj.* (NOO guh toh ree) or (NYOO guh toh ree) of little importance, ineffective, null

In trying to refute his opponents' claim that he was lacking in vision, the demagogue's partisan speech was so heavy-handed as to be *nugatory*.

At first, the scientist felt most of his theories were *nugatory*, and he refused to publish them. But as the importance of their conclusions became evident, he realized the danger of publication, and continued to keep them to himself.

NUMINOUS *adj.* (NOO muh nuhs) or (NYOO mun nuhs) related to a numen (a spirit said to inhabit natural objects); sacred; holy; spiritual

A *numen* is believed by animists to be a spirit that inhabits rocks, trees, or other natural phenomena. *Numinous* refers to the spiritual, non-rational aspects that are the basis of religion, the magical and majestic presence that can inspire awe or dread.

Even for a non-believer, there is a certain *numinous* quality to many pre-Renaissance icons that is immensely moving.

Much of the sixties' idealism is aimed at replacing materialism with more *numinous* concepts of love and spirituality.

NUMISMATICS *n.* (noo muhz MAD iks) the study of coins or currency; the collecting of coins or currency

Whenever she was confronted with her miserliness, she would insist that she studied *numismatics* and could not afford to give up even a penny lest it prove valuable.

OBJURGATE *v.* (AHB juhr gayt) to scold sharply

Although the candidate had no trouble *objurgating* his opponent, he was unable to offer any plan of his own.

Miller *objurgated* her husband for his habit of talking with his mouth full.

OBLOQUY *n.* (AHB luh kwee) abusive language, slander directed against a person; ill repute, the condition of one who has been slandered

He found the best way to cause trouble for his detractors was to ignore their *obloquy* and to continue as if nothing had been said.

Imagine our hero's surprise to find her name among those mentioned with *obloquy* by the fascist government.

OBSTREPEROUS *adj.* (uhbz TREP uh ruhs) stubbornly and loudly defiant; clamorous; unmanageable

This word suggests a loud and defiant unruliness directed against whoever is in charge.

Upon being told that they would have to leave, the crowd erupted in *obstreperous* roaring.

The minority faction is so *obstreperous* that they are often successful at ending any possibility of debate.

OCCAM'S RAZOR *n.* (AH kuhmz RAY zuhr) a theory in science and philosophy that when presented with two or more theories, the simplest should be considered the best, and that any new, unknown phenomenon can only be understood through that which is already understood.

If we apply *Occam's razor* to these theories, we will find that, as usual, the most straightforward explanation is correct.

QUICK QUIZ #39

Match each word in the first column with its definition in the second column. Check your answers in the back of the book.

1. Nimrod	a. calumny
2. nonplus	b. easiest is best
3. nostrum	c. defiant
4. nugatory	d. spiritual
5. numinous	e. to scold
6. numismatics	f. quack medicine
7. objurgate	g. bewilder
8. obloquy	h. hunter
9. obstreperous	i. coin collecting
10. Occam's razor	j. trifling

OEUVRE *n.* (EUVR) or (UHV) or (EEV ruh) the entire body of work of an artist; a work of art

The blockbuster exhibition of Picasso's work at the Metropolitan, poses the best chance of understanding the scale and diversity of this great artist's *oeuvre*.

Although his Ninth Symphony is the most popular in Beethoven's *oeuvre*, some of his lighter pieces are more brilliantly crafted.

OMBUDSMAN *n.* (AHM boodz muhn) or (AHM buhdz muhn) a man who mediates settlements between aggrieved parties, esp. representing people against the government; a mediator

An *ombudsman* is one who helps someone get redress when a government is following the law but still not serving the people.

After writing to the mayor and the local congressman to no avail, she took her cause to the head of the public watchdog committee, the official *ombudsman* of the city.

She was a self-proclaimed *ombudswoman* who would make every cause her personal vendetta.

OMPHALOSKEPSIS *n.* (ahm fuh loh SKEP sis) a meditation on one's navel practiced by Eastern mystics to achieve mystical fulfillment

From the Greek omphal (navel) and skepsis (viewing, examining), this word might just prove that there is an English word for every occasion. The word, although not useful except in rare occasions, might describe a more effective meditative technique if it implied that the practitioner was to concentrate on another's navel.

ONANISM *n.* (OHN uh niz uhm) coitus interuptus; masturbation; self-gratification

This word comes from Onan, a son of Judah, who disobeyed God and spilt his seed upon the ground rather than give his brother offspring. (Onan was convinced that the offspring would not be his, because he was with his brother's wife.)

Dorothy Parker is credited with naming her bird *Onan*. He was always spilling his seed on the ground.

Dire theories about the dangers of *onanism* have been prevalent for centuries.

The review degenerated into the solipsistic intellectual *onanism* that we have all learned to expect from him.

ONTOGENY n. (AHN tuh je nee) or (ahn tuh JE nee) the development of an organism from conception to adult

This word is often heard in the phrase "ontogeny recapitulates phylogeny," which stated that the development of an organism from conception mirrored its evolutionary development. A human embryo might represent a fish and then a monkey, etc.

Much insight can be gained into the development of man through a study of his *ontogeny*.

ONTOLOGY n. (auh TAHL uh jee) the philosophical study of the nature of being

Ontology, the study of being, was first used by scholastic writers of the seventeenth century. An *ontological* argument for the existence of God, however, was presented in the eleventh century by Anselm who stated that since God was perfect, he must exist. A being that did not exist would not be perfect. This tautology was exploded by Immanuel Kant who argued that something can only exist if its existence can be tested and proven.

Another *ontological* philosopher was Martin Heidegger, who found that being and nothing are opposites that together make up a whole. Because humans live on the cusp of these two concepts, our lives are full of metaphysical angst.

ONUS n. (OH nuhs) burden, something that takes considerable effort to accomplish; blame

Onus is sometimes used in the phrase "onus probandi" (OH nuhs proh BAN dye) which means burden of proof. In recent years, it has been satisfactory to just use *onus* for short.

The accused used a clever dodge to get acquitted; he shifted the *onus* onto the victim who had to beg to be spared prosecution.

OPISTHENAR n. (uh PIS thuh nahr) back of the hand

From the Greek opisth (back) and thenar (hand), this is the medical term for the back of the hand, but for us laymen, it can serve as a pretentious way of phrasing an old saying:

I know it like my *opisthenar*.

OPUS n. (OH puhs) a creative work

Opus is usually used by itself to distinguish between different classical pieces of music in a composer's oeuvre, but the word is often seen in combination as "magnum opus" (MAG nuhm OH puhs), a great work.

Moviegoers hated the director's latest film, although he considered it his magnum *opus*.

OSSIFY *v.* (AH suh fye) to become bone; to become rigidly conventional, to mold into a conventional pattern.

As a child develops to maturity, some of the cartilage around his nose *ossifies*.

We had watched professor after professor gain tenure and become *ossified*. The only way to keep new ideas flowing into this institution is to enforce a retirement age of thirty-five.

QUICK QUIZ #40

Match each word in the first column with its definition in the second column. Check your answers in the back of the book.

1.	oeuvre	a.	masturbation
2.	ombudsman	b.	creative work
3.	omphaloskepsis	c.	study of being
4.	onanism	d.	become bony
5.	ontogeny	e.	mediator
6.	ontology	f.	back of the hand
7.	onus	g.	artist's work
8.	opisthenar	h.	burden
9.	opus	i.	organismic development
10.	ossify	j.	navel meditating

OTIOSE *adj.* (OH shee ohs) or (OHT ee ohs) lazy; useless; futile

Something that is *otiose* can be somewhere between superfluous and downright wasteful.

Our relationship with Taiwan has degenerated from an active to an *otiose* support of its capitalist government.

The play, while expertly crafted, contains some *otiose* lines that, if removed, would make it perfect.

Trying to get a cat to jump through hoops is an *otiose* undertaking.

OUBLIETTE *n.* (oo blee ET) a dungeon which has only one exit, a trap door in its roof

This word comes from the French oublier (to forget) and undoubtedly one thrown into an oubliette was put there so that he might be forgotten.

Her once trustworthy servant had been thrust away in the *oubliette* for trying to surreptitiously spit in her soup.

Our society would like nothing better than to throw its criminals into an *oubliette* where they could do no harm and would eventually starve to death.

OUTRÊ *adj.* (oo TRAY) eccentric to the point of deviance, bizarre, extravagant

Monty Python came about at a time when such brazenly physical comedy was *outré* enough to shock and amuse an entire generation of college students and cult-film addicts.

PABLUM *n.* (PAB luhm) a cereal for infants patented in 1932; something made palatable

The problem with the previous curriculum is that it reduced a complex and exciting history to a *pablum* of names and dates.

The museum's images of the destruction of native American society were as palatable as *pablum*, and thus, did not serve to teach viewers of the atrocities committed by the nineteenth century U.S. government.

PABULUM *n.* (PAB yuh luhm) that which nourishes or feeds; often used figuratively. i.e. "food for the mind"

Pabulum, when used to describe food, usually refers to that taken in by animal organs or plants, especially when it is in a liquid form that allows for easy transfer through a cell membrane or wall. When it is used figuratively, it can sometimes refer to an insipid piece of writing, as if reduced to a liquid form suitable to plants.

The human body converts food to glucose which enters the bloodstream. This *pabulum* is then absorbed by the organs which use it for energy.

He was surprised that such an intelligent person would like the sentimental *pabulum* passed off by that so-called author as original.

PACE *prep.* (PAY see) or (PAH chay) with deference to

This word, the singular of pax (peace), is used when an author wants to indicate polite disagreement. It is sometimes used ironically.

"I have not, *pace* the press," said the famous supermodel, "had any clandestine relationship with the President, the first lady, the first cat, or the first valet."

I do not, *pace* the social biologists, believe that genetics has anything to do with what is happening in our poorer communities.

PAEAN *adj.* (PAY ahn) an intensely joyous hymn, a jubilant outburst (also pean)

Paean is another name for Apollo, the great god of archery, prophecy, music, and healing who became the sun god. Consequently, the word is used to describe a hymn to Apollo, and today, any joyous song or hymn.

The fans stood with hand on heart and sang *The Star Spangled Banner*, a great *paean* to liberty, before their heroes began to punch each other senseless.

When the movie star reappeared on the screen, onscreen cheering rose to a *paean* of adulation.

PALAVER *n.* (puh LAV uhr) a long meeting or conference; idle chitchat; talk meant to charm *v.* to cajole, to wheedle; to partake of idle chitchat

This word was originally used by Portuguese sailors in Africa to describe a long parley between the indigenous populations and the Europeans. It was then picked up by English sailors who brought the word to landlubbers who liked it enough to use it.

The heads of the players' union and a representative from the owners engaged in a three-week *palaver* to no avail.

Don't waste your *palaver* on me. I am a busy man with many more important things to do than listen to you.

PALIMPSEST *n.* (PAL imp sest) parchment or other writing surface, from which something has been erased, and then reused for something else; a brass plate which has been turned so that its former message faces the wall

Historians have been surprisingly successful at deciphering ancient *palimpsests*, discovering obscure treasures as well as laundry lists and other detritus of history beneath the manuscripts of a later generation.

PALINDROME *n.* (PAL in drohm) a word whose letters spell the same thing forward and backwards. The following are all examples of *palindromes*:

Anna
redivider
A man, a plan, a canal, Panama
Able was I ere I saw Elba
Lewd did I live, evil I did dwel
Madam, I'm Adam
Sex at noon taxes

Quick Quiz #41

Match each word in the first column with its definition in the second column. Check your answers in the back of the book.

1. otiose	a. something nourishing
2. oubliette	b. eccentric
3. outré	c. with deference to
4. pablum	d. erased parchment
5. pabulum	e. word is same backwards
6. pace	f. meeting
7. paean	g. baby gruel
8. palaver	h. dungeon
9. palimpsest	i. lazy, useless
10. palindrome	j. joyous outburst

PANACHE *n.* (puh NASH) verve; style; a plume of feathers, esp. on a helmet

Although clumsy and shy about most of his activities, Billy could play the piano with *panache*.

PANGLOSSIAN *adj.* (pan GLAHS ee uhn) stupidly or naively optimistic

This word comes from Pangloss, an optimistic tutor from Voltaire's *Candide*, who believes that "all is for the best in the best of all possible worlds." *Panglossian* describes one who is optimistic to an absurd degree, who believes that no matter what happens, it will lead to some good.

PANJANDRUM *n.* (pan JAN druhm) a self-important person

Playwright Samuel Foote first invented panjandrum in 1755 as part of line of nonsense used to challenge the memory of a character who claimed to be able to repeat anything upon hearing it just once. The word today is used as a mock title for someone who is a pompous pretender to power.

Councilperson Presley, a *panjandrum* of local politics, spent most of his time in the council pontificating on the merits of belonging to the council.

PANTHEISM *n.* (PAN thee iz uhm) the belief that God is everything in the universe and that the universe is all God

Pantheists, similar to atheists in that they believe that there is no transcendent God, believe that universe and its laws are the only God.

Murphy believed in *pantheism*, and as such, he did not practice any religion but that of science.

PANTHEON *n.* (PAN thee ahn) a Roman temple built in 27 B.C. that is circular and meant to honor all of the gods; all the gods of a people; a group of people who are considered major contributors to a field

Although you may see this word used to describe a temple to all the gods, you are most likely to see it meaning a group of god-like contributors to a field who are held in the highest esteem.

Chuck Jones, who made Bugs Bunny and other great characters famous, occupies a respected place in the *pantheon* of cartoonists.

Lamaark, whose theory of gradualism had been discredited for years, has recently retaken his place in the *pantheon* of evolutionary biology.

PARAMOUR *n.* (PAR uh moor) or (PAR uh mohr) a lover, esp. an illicit lover

Her husband left the house on some alleged business or other, but she had no doubt that he was off to see his *paramour*.

At first the police could determine no motive for the killing, but they then realized that one suspect had been the husband's *paramour*.

PARLANCE *n.* (PAHR luhnss) a manner of speaking, diction, idiom, phraseology; a speech, an instance of speaking

Court TV has brought many examples of legal *parlance* into the mainstream.

PARONOMASIA *n.* (par uh noh MAY zyuh) a pun or punning

Even the title of Julian Sharman's *A Cursory History of Swearing* is a *paronomasia*.

Chef Louis said *paronomasically* "This roast chicken would have been tasty, but for a little more thyme (time)."

PARVENU *n.* (PAHR vuh noo) or (pahv uh NOO) an upstart who has suddenly acquired wealth or prestige but is not accepted socially by others in his new class *adj.* like a parvenu

The committee was forced to accept two new members who were nothing but loud-mouthed *parvenus* willing to do anything to make it seem as if they had been rich for generations.

It is surprising that in one generation a family can move from being *parvenus* to being part of the accepted gentry.

PASQUINADE *n.* (pas kwuh NAYD) a satire that ridicules a specific person, traditionally posted in public *v.* to ridicule through posting a pasquinade

This word comes from Pasquin, the torso of an ancient statue dug up in 1501 and placed in a Roman plaza by a Cardinal Caraffa. He decided that it would be good fun to dress up the ancient marble in fancy clothes to resemble an ancient mythological figure. As an intellectual exercise, or perhaps for the sheer fun of it, the students and professors of the local school of Ancient Learning posted odes to Pasquin on the statue. As time went on, these pasquinades became more and more satirical, and the word began to be used to describe any satirical writing or lampoon aimed at a particular person.

QUICK QUIZ #42

Match each word in the first column with its definition in the second column. *Check your answers in the back of the book.*

1. panache	a. diction
2. Panglossian	b. lover
3. panjandrum	c. self-important person
4. pantheism	d. all the gods
5. pantheon	e. social climber
6. paramour	f. belief in all gods
7. parlance	g. pun
8. paronomasia	h. verve
9. parvenu	i. optimistic
10. pasquinade	j. satire

PASTICHE *n.* (pa STEESH) a satirical, dramatic, literary, or musical piece that imitates, usually deliberately, the works of others with sardonic intent; a farrago, a hodgepodge from different sources

This word comes from the Italian *pasticcio,* a pie made with many ingredients, and has since, like farrago, olla podrida, salmagundi, and oleo, come to mean a hodgepodge of different ingredients that form something else.

Star Wars, a *pastiche* of the old *Flash Gordon* TV series and B-movie fare, became one of the most popular movies ever made.

Why go to Orlando to see a *pastiche* of German architecture when you can go to see the real thing in the small towns of Germany?

PATHETIC FALLACY *n.* (puh THED ik FAL luh see) ascribing human emotions to inanimate objects or nature

This phrase was coined by art historian John Ruskin to describe applying human emotions to natural objects. Another word used to describe the same phenomenon is anthropomorphism.

The following sentence is replete with examples of the *pathetic fallacy*: He escaped the violent downpour coming from the angry clouds, but the cruel wind was too much for him, and he succumbed to the heartless storm, drowning in the blood-sucking sea.

PATHOS *n.* (PAY thahs) that which in art arouses sympathy or pity or sorrow; the feeling of sympathy generated by pathos in art

The actor spoke of his time alone at sea with such *pathos* that there was not a dry eye in the house.

PATOIS *n.* (PA twah) a regional dialect of a language that differs from standard or literary speech; the language used by a particular group, jargon

Most speakers of American English have a hard time understanding the *patois* spoken on the island of Jamaica.

PECULATE *v.* (PEK yuh layt) to embezzle money

He started his business with a large sum *peculated* from the bank where he had worked as treasurer.

The company folded because its accountant had been *peculating* for years.

PEDAGOGUE *n.* (PED uh gahg) a schoolmaster, a teacher of children

This word implies a *pedantry* or dogmatism that one might expect in a tutor. It is related to the word *pedagogy* which describes the science of teaching.

The lecturer was adroit at getting his point across. He chose his words carefully, but showed none of the tone one might expect from a *pedagogue*.

Annoyed by the piddling *pedagogy* of the headmaster, the students revolted by stealing his shorts and running them up the flagpole.

Her methods unconventional, she was an excellent teacher, blissfully unaware of the science of *pedagogy*.

PEEN *n.* (PEEN) the end of the hammer opposite the face (not the claw, but a ball shaped part for hammering) (also *pean*) *v.* to flatten metal using a peen

To get that nail to go in straight you'd better use the *peen* of the hammer, not the claw.

PELLUCID *adj.* (puh LOO sid) intensely clear; easily understood

The tropical ocean near Key West was perfectly *pellucid*; every detail of the coral ten feet down could be seen as if no water was obscuring the view.

It was such a joy to read Hemingway's *pellucid* prose after fighting my way through Hegel's turgid treatise on existentialism.

After reading the doctor's unintelligible scrawl for years, the pharmacist was pleased that she had hired an amanuensis with *pellucid* handwriting.

PENULTIMATE *adj.* (pi NUHLT uh mit) next to last (also *penult*)

This word comes from the Latin pene (almost) combined with ultimate.

The *penultimate* chapter of the book should have been the last, which was otiose.

PENUMBRA *n.* (pi NUHM bruh) a partially shaded area in an eclipse (usually) between full sun and full shade; an area where something exists in an uncertain degree, fringe

Although we detected a slight change in the sun's brightness, we were only in the *penumbra* of the eclipse and certainly missed the excitement of a total eclipse.

The recent findings concerning the manner in which the HIV virus affects some people more quickly than others, while hopeful, exist in a *penumbra* of uncertainty that seems almost impervious to study.

Quick Quiz #43

Match each word in the first column with its definition in the second column. Check your answers in the back of the book.

1. pastiche	a. shadow
2. pathetic fallacy	b. anthropomorphism
3. pathos	c. dialect
4. patois	d. a teacher
5. peculate	e. clear
6. pedagogue	f. embezzle
7. peen	g. next to last
8. pellucid	h. satirical piece
9. penultimate	i. ball shaped end of hammer
10. penumbra	j. something that arrouses sympathy

PENURIOUS *adj.* (pi NOO ree uhs) stingy, unwilling to part with money, mean-spiritedly parsimonious; poor, poverty-stricken

The successful entrepreneur, while generous in giving to charities, was *penurious* in his salaries to his employees.

The drought made it even harder to grow anything from the *penurious* land surrounding the desert.

PERDITION *n.* (puhr DI shun) eternal damnation

It remains to be seen whether those who voted for the Satanist candidate in the last election have earned themselves *perdition*.

PERORATE *v.* (PER uh rayt) or (per oh RAYT) to make a long speech, esp. in a grandiloquent manner; to sum up a speech

Numerous supporters prattled on at length, but there was nobody to *perorate* against the proposal to raise taxes for the poor.

The politician spoke at length on the situation and then *perorated* with a great flourish.

PERSIFLAGE *n.* (PUHR suh flahzh) or (per suh FLAHZH) banter; a frivolous manner of treating a subject

When the talk turned to money, his smooth and meaningless *persiflage* ceased abruptly, and he listened attentively.

She had been seated next to a fop who was the consummate *persifleur*; she tried everything that a polite woman could to free herself from the situation, but had to resort to insulting his clothing to get him to shut up.

PERTINACIOUS *adj.* (PUHR tuhn ay shuhs) or (purh tuhn AY shuhs) that holds stubbornly and tenaciously to a course of action; perversely persistent

His sleep was disturbed by a *pertinacious* mosquito who must have drained a gallon of blood.

Children are endowed with a *pertinacious* curiosity that if not quelled can lead to a lifelong love of learning.

PETTIFOGGER *n.* (PET ee fah guhr) a disreputable lawyer who works mainly on petty cases; one who worries over trivial details

His leg crushed by a careless truck driver, Bart could not decide which was worse, the wheedling insurance agent from the trucking company, or the rapscallion *pettifoggers* who kept showing up unannounced to his hospital room.

A *pettifogger* by nature, Sarita almost refused the hundred dollar bill because of a small rip in its corner.

PHARISIACAL *adj.* (far uh SAY ik uhl) or (FAR uh say ik uhl) relating to the Pharisees; hypocritical (also *pharisaic* [far uh SAY ik] or [FAR uh say ik])

This word comes from the Pharisees, an ancient Jewish sect described in the Bible as sanctimonious, hypocritical and self-righteous. The Pharisees are constantly questioning Jesus as to whether he is doing the correct thing.

Her fiancé's criticisms of her lifestyle seemed outlandishly *pharisaical*; he accused her of sins that he himself often committed.

In suggesting that many need to be more considerate of others, we include ourselves to avoid being *pharisaical*.

PHENOMENOLOGY *n.* (fi nawm uh NAWL oh jee) a philosophical theory based on the idea that phenomena should only be experienced subjectively through intuition, that any attempt at rational analysis of facts can get in the way of understanding

Phenomenology, founded by German philosopher Edmund Husserl (1859-1938), is a theory that attempts to relate a person to her external world. A *phenomenologist* is not just a thinking being but is one who is conscious that she is conscious, and can step out of herself to reflect on her experience. She does not just experience something, she actually adds her values and feelings to the act of experimenting in a process called *intentionality*. *Phenomenology* seeks to make intuition the primary method of gaining knowledge.

PHILIPPIC *n.* (fi LIP ik) tirade, an attack

This word comes from speeches given by Demosthenes who succeeded in convincing the Athenians to fight against Philip of Macedon. A *philippic* is a speech that can rile up its audience against someone.

The President, in seeking to rouse the nation, pronounced bitter *philippics* against the USSR.

PHLEGMATIC *adj.* (fleg MAT ik) calm, composed

Early practitioners of physiology believed that there were four humors—black bile, blood, yellow bile, and phlegm—that made up the body and their relative proportion would determine a person's health and temperament. Black bile made a person gloomy, blood tended to represent sanguinity and cheerfulness, yellow bile, irascibility, and phlegm, sluggishness. *Phlegm* (FLEM), which described the mucus in our respiratory system, is still used to describe an apathetic person, and *phlegmatic* means marked by slowness or impassivity.

While her suitor hammered on the door and screamed passionately, the *phlegmatic* heiress locked the door and returned to her napping.

QUICK QUIZ #44

Match each word in the first column with its definition in the second column. Check your answers in the back of the book.

1. penurious	a. quibbling lawyer
2. perdition	b. hypercritical
3. perorate	c. tirade
4. persiflage	d. make a long speech
5. pertinacious	e. obstinate
6. pettifogger	f. banter
7. pharisaical	g. poor
8. phenomenology	h. philosophy of intuition
9. Philippic	i. damnation
10. phlegmatic	j. calm

PHYLOGENY *n.* (fye LAH juh nee) the evolutionary development of a species; the evolutionary development of a part of an organism

Darwin arrived at his theory of evolution through an investigation of the *phylogeny* of Galapagos chicks.

The *phylogeny* of a few of the bones in the wrist is still unknown.

Evolutionary biology has become so specialized that some scientists spend an entire career studying the *phylogeny* of the eye of an obscure reptile.

PICAYUNE *n.* (pik ee YOON) or (PIK ee yoon) a Spanish coin worth about six cents and used in the Southern U.S. in the nineteenth century; something of the least value *adj.* paltry, trivial; petty

He was constantly reminding us how everyone had told him that his now-valuable real estate was not worth a *picayune*.

Compared to the vast amount spent on the military, any savings resulting from cutbacks in the arts are *picayune*.

PILCROW *n.* (PIL kroh) ¶; the paragraph symbol

The editor placed a *pilcrow* where she thought a new paragraph should begin.

PILLORY *n.* (PIL or ee) a post with a wooden crosspiece with holes for head and hands in which prisoners were made to stand outside to be subject to the public's scorn *v.* to expose to public contempt or ridicule; to punish by putting in the pillory

For leering at the governor's wife, Hawthorne was placed in the *pillory* for six hours.

For his careless comment about the need to reduce Social Security benefits, the President's economic adviser was *pilloried* in the press.

PINGUID *adj.* (PING wid) fat; unctuous

Her toe might not have been broken had the *pinguid* swine who stepped on it had fewer between-meal snacks.

PLANGENT *adj.* (PLAN juhnt) loud and resonant; or expressing sadness

It was impossible for the quarterback to be heard over the *plangent* roar of the crowd.

The symphony's third movement was simple and rhythmic except for the *plangent* tones of a lone oboist who carried the melody.

PLENARY *adj.* (PLEE nuh ree) or (PLEN uh ree) complete or full, not deficient in any area; fully attended by all who are entitled

Although the chairwoman could not attend the event, she gave her associate *plenary* powers to handle the situation.

The decision to raise taxes was made during a rare *plenary* session of the House of Representatives.

PLENIPOTENTIARY *adj.* (plen uh puh TEN chuh ree) or (PLEN uh puh ten chuh ree) given full authority or power *n.* a diplomat given full authorization to transact any business

This word is sometimes used after the noun it modifies when describing an ambassador, a minister or an envoy who is given full authority.

Franklin, acting as minister *plenipotentiary* for the United States, made his own decision when offered the entire area of Louisiana by the French.

PLEONASM *n.* (PLE uh naz uhm) the use of an excess of words to express an idea when only a few words would make the same statement clear to anyone who could see with his own eyes; superfluity

The warmth of their greeting was enough, the kiss on the lips a *pleonasm*.

PLUVIOUS *n.* (PLOO vee uhs) rainy, marked by heavy rainfall

The *pluvious* weather had continued for over three weeks and was beginning to worry the farmers whose fields were becoming lakes.

QUICK QUIZ #45

Match each word in the first column with its definition in the second column. Check your answers in the back of the book.

1.	phylogeny	a.	rainy
2.	picayune	b.	¶
3.	pilcrow	c.	redundancy
4.	pillory	d.	tiny
5.	pinguid	e.	oily
6.	plangent	f.	full
7.	plenary	g.	having complete powers
8.	plenipotentiary	h.	development of a species
9.	pleonasm	i.	loud
10.	pluvious	j.	ridicule

POLITIC *adj.* (PAH luh tik) shrewd, diplomatic, careful; judicious; crafty, expedient

This word suggests a shrewd handling of people through use of diplomacy or other wheedling techniques. It can also mean what is judicious in arriving at a diplomatic goal, even if unethical means are used.

It would not be *politic* to tell the truth about the boss's bad taste in clothing.

Upon being asked to give the golden apple to the fairest of the three goddesses, Paris was not *politic*; he made a choice.

POLLYANNA *n.* (pah lee AN nuh) one who is unduly optimistic

This word comes from the children's stories of Eleanor Hodgman Porter (1868-1920), who wrote of a character named Pollyanna Whittier who was happy in any circumstance, often foolishly so.

For professing a belief in the possibility of balancing the deficit in only two years, Senator Bott was accused of being a *Pollyanna*.

Her theory that their love might bloom again was *Pollyannaish*.

POLTROON *n.* (pahl TROON) craven, a coward

Etymologists used to theorize that this word came from the Latin *pollice truncus*, 'maimed or mutilated in the thumb.' A coward might cut off his thumb to avoid military service. Today's lexicographers have pretty much discredited this theory.

A pusillanimous *poltroon*, he was afraid to even get out of bed in the morning and jumped at the slightest noise.

PONIARD *n.* (PAHN yuhrd) a dagger with a thin triangular or square blade *v.* to stab with a poniard

The thrust of the assassin's *poniard* came too late to stop the double agent from spilling his guts.

Afraid for their lives, the outlaws walked lightly, prepared to *poniard* anyone who got in their way.

POPINJAY *n.* (PAH pin jay) a vain person who talks a lot

This word originally meant a parrot, but it now almost exclusively refers to a person who has parrot-like qualities. He may talk a lot or wear ostentatious clothing or might be simply vain.

Stuck in an elevator with a *popinjay*, Melissa passed the time by counting and re-counting the gleaming buttons on the front of his shirt.

PORTMANTEAU *n.* (pohrt MANT oh) a large suitcase; a portmanteau word is a word made from two other words by combining sounds; e.g. smog

The second meaning of this word was first applied by Lewis Carroll in *Through the Looking Glass*:

"That'll do very well," said Alice, "and 'slithy'?"

"Well, 'slithy' means lithe and slimy. 'Lithe' is the same as 'active.' You see it's like a portmanteau—there are two meanings packed up into one word."

—from *Through the Looking-Glass*, by Lewis Carroll

POSIT *v.* (PAH zit) to postulate or theorize, to assume to be true; to place in position

In the absence of clear evidence, the prosecutor began by *positing* that someone close to the family must have been involved in the crime. She then made her case by arguing that the accused was the only one still alive with any connections to the family.

The participants at the seance watched in awe as heavy objects floated and were then *posited* by some unseen force.

POSITIVISM *n.* (PAHZ it i viz uhm) the philosophical theory that only sense perceptions can be used for precise thought, similar to empiricism

Positivism, invented by Auguste Comte (1798-1857), is the philosophical theory behind the scientific method. A *positivist* recognizes only observable phenomena, throwing any inquiry about causes or purpose into the trash heap of philosophical reasoning.

POULTICE *n.* (POL tis) a moist mass of matter (bread, meal or clay) applied externally to soothe an aching part of the body *v.* to apply a poultice to

In the eighteenth century, medical providers would apply *poultices* constructed of the oddest ingredients to help cure minor injuries. One cure for boils included a *poultice* of raisins, hog's lard, or honey. If it didn't cure the boils, it might provide someone with a handy lunch.

Dweezil's pockmarked complexion was brought on by continuous *poulticing*.

PRANDIAL *adj.* (PRAN dee uhl) related to a meal

This word is usually used in combination with pre or post.

His illness could not be traced to the previous day's heavy meals, but rather to the excessive *postprandial* potations.

He could barely stay awake during dinner, and now he had to deal with three hours of *postprandial* oratory.

QUICK QUIZ #46

Match each word in the first column to its definition in the second column. Check your answers in the back of the book.

1.	politic	a.	suitcase
2.	Pollyanna	b.	postulate
3.	poltroon	c.	gunk used to heal
4.	poniard	d.	empiricism
5.	popinjay	e.	optimist
6.	portmanteau	f.	vain talker
7.	posit	g.	coward
8.	positivism	h.	shrewd
9.	poultice	i.	dagger
10.	prandial	j.	related to a meal

PRÉCIS *n.* (pray SEE) a summary of a work; an abstract

The author had constructed a *précis* of American history that was under fifty pages long.

One could gain an almost complete understanding of her discourse through reading the *précis*. The body of the text, in fact, was turgid and uninformative.

PREDICATE *v.* (PRED uh kayt) to establish, to base; to affirm, to declare; to ascribe a quality to (used with of)

The prosecutor *predicated* his argument on circumstantial evidence that was nonetheless capable of convincing the jury of the accused's guilt.

Jefferson *predicated* the freedom of man in the preamble to the Constitution.

PRESTIDIGITION *n.* (pres tuh dij uh TAY shun) the execution of tricks through sleight of hand; legerdemain

This word is a combination of the Italian "presto" (presto) and the Latin "digit-us" (finger). It is used figuratively.

Maurice is a type of Epicurean *prestidigitator*, able to eat five separate meals at one time and keep track of the separate tastes of each of them.

PRIAPIC *adj.* (prye A pik) phallic; suggesting a phallus

This word comes from Priapus (prye AY puhs), the ancient god of procreation. Statues of Priapus were placed in gardens where they were used to increase yields and to scare birds.

The *priapic* missile rocketing out of its silo was enough to send General Gureasmo into paroxysms of delight. He said, "The world, ahem war, is over."

The artwork featured a *priapic* silhouette of a soldier that moved up and down with the help of a hidden motor.

PRIG *n.* (PRIG) one who is arrogantly pedantic or moral, and whose attitude bores others

Just our luck to have a principal who, as a conscientious *prig* of the old school, required uniforms and a "yes ma'am" from everybody.

PRIMOGENITURE *n.* (prye moh JEN uh choor) the state of being the first born; the right to inherit given to the eldest son

From a study of the Bible it is clear that *primogeniture* was important, but only if the first born child was a man.

Easu gave up his right of *primogeniture* for a bowl of pottage.

PROBITY *n.* (PROH buht ee) honesty, uprightness, integrity

The judge was a woman of indisputable *probity*; no one had even attempted to bribe her.

The senator, a rare politician of *probity*, declared that the death penalty would not lower crime rates.

PROCLIVITY *n.* (proh KLIV uht ee) a tendency or inclination, predisposition

This word often refers to a general tendency toward something that is negative and should be avoided, but which is difficult to avoid because of habit or temperament.

It's not a good idea to force someone into a career for which he has no *proclivity*.

Marie's *proclivity* for gossip kept us well informed, but also discouraged us from sharing secrets with her.

PROCRUSTEAN *adj.* (proh KRUHS tee uhn) designed to exact strict conformity without regard for individual differences

This word comes from Procrustes, a giant of Attica who would grab any travelers who passed his way and force them into an iron bed. If they were too small, he stretched them to fit, if too large, he cut off their limbs. In the end, Procrustes was killed by Theseus, who forced him into a bed of his own.

The newly passed *Procrustean* legislation forced people to conform their lives to rigid laws in order to get benefits.

She had *Procrustean* standards for friendship. If she couldn't change a friend's priorities to the point where they were acceptable, she found another friend.

PROGNATHOUS *adj.* (PRAHG nuh thuhs) protruding; a jaw that projects in front of the face

When she turned her head, I noticed a *prognathous* jaw that gave her a look of determination.

QUICK QUIZ #47

Match each word in the first column to its definition in the second column. Check your answers in the back of the book.

1. précis	a. abstract
2. predicate	b. phallic
3. prestidigitation	c. requiring strict conformity
4. priapic	d. pedant
5. prig	e. tendency
6. primogeniture	f. sleight of hand
7. probity	g. honesty
8. proclivity	h. first born
9. Procrustean	i. protruding
10. prognathous	j. establish

PROGNOSTICATE *v.* (prahg NAHS tuh kayt) to predict; foreshadow, presage

It was easy for any shrewd man to *prognosticate* the fate of the plan to lower taxes. It was doomed to failure before it began.

The colder than usual autumn and the early snow both *prognosticated* a difficult winter.

PROLIX *adj.* (proh LIKS) tediously wordy, unusually long; tending to speak or write in such a manner

His ideas were well thought-out, but his prose was *prolix*, and had to be ruthlessly edited.

Most academic studies suffer from a writing style that is windy and *prolix*.

The commencement speaker, unfortunately for the hungry graduates, was *prolix*, holding forth on the merits of good grammar for two hours.

PROPHYLAXIS *n.* (proh fuh LAK sis) the prevention or protection from disease

Standard medical school teaches doctors to treat disease, but there is little emphasis on *prophylaxis*.

PROPINQUITY *n.* (proh PINK wuhd ee) nearness; having a close familial relationship to

To avoid fetid odors, a compost pile should not be placed in close *propinquity* to the house.

The two cousins on opposite sides of the family were of the same degree of *propinquity* to their rich uncle.

PROTEAN *adj.* (PROH tee ahn) or (PROHD ee uhn) taking on various shapes or forms; exhibiting variety

This word comes from Proteus, an ancient sea god who could change shapes at will.

The flower was of a *protean* hue that appeared to be reddish when seen in direct sun, and pale pink when seen at twilight.

An actor of *protean* talents, Barrymore could play Shakespeare as well as Vaudeville.

Her personality is so complex, so *protean*, that any attempt to pigeonhole her would be impossible.

PROVENANCE *n.* (PRAHV uh nuhns) origin, derivation; proof of past ownership (for antiques or fine art)

The *provenance* of the apples that seemed fresh in May must have been somewhere south of the equator.

She bought the painting of Italian *provenance* in Brazil, where its owner had fled after some shady dealings in Sicily.

The gallery owner wanted a *provenance* of the painting to prove that it was really a Picasso.

PSEPHOLOGY *n.* (see FAHL uh jee) the study of elections

This word, coined in the fifties, is derived from the Greek word psephos, meaning pebble. It seems that people used to drop colored pebbles in a box to register their votes.

Through applying the science of *psephology*, it is clear that the incumbents have no mandate to pursue any legislative agenda.

PUCE *n.* (PYOOS) a gray brownish purple

This word comes from the Latin pu-lex (flea). Puce is a dark red, almost purple, slightly gray color.

Not only had she made the mistake of wearing *puce* in December, but she had attended a ball where everyone else was wearing black.

PUDENCY *n.* (PYOO duhn see) modesty, prudishness

Her *pudency* was apparent in her clothing, which was not low-cut, and in her modest habit of covering her mouth when she laughed.

PUERILE *adj.* (PYOO ruhl) or (PYOO ryel) juvenile; immature, puerilely *adv.* (PYOO ruhl lee)

His writing, while not so poorly constructed, expressed *puerile* ideas that were inconsistent with his stature as a tenured professor.

The normally mature and eloquent senators descended into a *puerile* blather when confronted with evidence of unethical campaign contributions.

QUICK QUIZ #48

Match each word in the first column with its definition in the second column. Check your answers in the back of the book.

1. prognosticate	a. study of elections
2. prolix	b. proximity
3. prophylaxis	c. origin
4. propinquity	d. modesty
5. protean	e. wordy
6. provenance	f. predict
7. psephology	g. prevention of disease
8. puce	h. taking on many shapes
9. pudency	i. gray purple
10. puerile	j. juvenile

PUISSANCE n. (PYOO uhs uhns) or (PYOO is uhns) or (PWIS suhns) power, strength

While legislators will chop a social program in half at the drop of a hat, they leave the gun control programs alone for fear of the *puissance* of the NRA.

The king had no choice but to bow to the *puissance* of Parliament and sign the Magna Carta.

PULCHRITUDE n. (PUHL kruh tood) physical beauty

Although of no great *pulchritude*, Morton had no trouble finding dates because of his winning personality.

PURVIEW n. (PUHR vyoo) scope, range; range of vision or comprehension

The troubles we had with the U.S. post office were ostensibly outside the *purview* of the local postmaster, who said her job was not to remedy problems.

Randall's home, nestled in a dingle, was well within the *purview* of the scenic overlook, and had therefore been included in many tourists' snapshots of the valley.

PUSILLANIMOUS adj. (pyoo suh LAN uh muhs) cowardly

This word comes from pusillus (very small, petty) and animus (soul, mind) and it implies a contemptible cowardliness.

Bad Bill Bigsby's decision to use his pregnant wife as a shield when facing the police was one of the meanest and most *pusillanimous* actions in local history.

The U.S.'s decision to avoid the conflict in the Balkans reeked of a selfish *pusillanimity* that belies our historical status as a helper to the poor and downtrodden.

PUTSCH n. (PEUTSH) (Rhymes with butch) an attempt at overthrowing a government swiftly that is planned in secret.

A putsch is different from a coup d'état (koo day TAH) in that a coup is successful, while a putsch is just an attempt at a coup d'état. George Johnson, history teacher, defined a putsch as "a coup d'état that went kaput." Perhaps the most famous putsch, the Bierhall Putsch of 1923, was led by Hitler and resulted in his imprisonment, during which he wrote *Mien Kamf*.

Up to the day in which it was attempted, the *Putsch* of former USSR military leaders was kept secret from the presiding government.

PYRRHIC adj. (PIR ik) relating to Pyrrhus, king of Epirus

A Pyrrhic victory is one that is too costly. This meaning comes from Pyrrhus's victory over the Romans at Aseulum in 279 B.C. Although Pyrrhus's army was successful in routing the Romans, his losses were severe.

Although the young emergency-room doctor had succeeded in bringing his patient back from the dead, it was a *Pyrrhic* victory. In the time during which the patient's heart was not functioning, severe liver damage had resulted.

QUA prep. (KWAH) or (KWAY) in the capacity or role of

The Democratic senators' criticisms are not against the President *qua* commander-in-chief, but rather against the President *qua* head of the Democratic party.

Some feminists believe that women *qua* women have certain responsibilities that differ from those of women *qua* breadwinners.

QUAFF v. (KWAHF) to drink deeply; to drink of a liquid freely. n. a drink quaffed

The pitcher of beer set down in the middle of the table was an invitation for all to *quaff* in celebration of the end of another hard day of work.

QUAGMIRE n. (KWAG myer) shaky boggy ground that gives under one's feet; a tough situation, a predicament

The floods in California have turned the entire state into a *quagmire*.

The first European arrivals in Florida faced the Herculean task of hacking through spiky palmetto palms. In addition, they had to avoid sinking into the numerous *quagmires* that dotted the land.

QUIDDITY n. (KWID uhd ee) the essence of something, that which makes it what it is; a quibble, a trivial distinction; a tendency to make trivial distinctions

The second meaning of this word, a trivial distinction, is derived from the quibbling arguments of the scholastics who would write at length on the *quiddity* of "things."

The *quiddity* of both recent Supreme Court decisions on search and seizure was that the government was violating the defendants' civil rights.

Aristotle argued that the *quiddity* of tragedy is its capacity to cause catharsis.

Her love was complete. She loved his physical being as well as every quirk and *quiddity* of his personality.

QUICK QUIZ #49

Match each word in the first column with its definition in the second column. Check your answers in the back of the book.

1. puissance	a. a costly victory
2. pulchritude	b. power
3. purview	c. drink
4. pusillanimous	d. range
5. putsch	e. essense
6. Pyrrhic	f. coup
7. qua	g. wimpy
8. quaff	h. bog
9. quagmire	i. in the capacity of
10. quiddity	j. beauty

QUIDNUNC *n.* (KWID nuhngk) a busybody, one who needs to know everything

This word comes from the Latin "quid" (what) and "nunc" (now), and it describes a person who is always demanding to know "what now?" or "what's up?"

Rock Star Blimpton's implication in the killing of his wife has put the *quidnuncs* of the world into a frenzy of speculation.

QUISLING *n.* (KWIZ ling) a traitor who betrays his own country by helping an enemy who occupies his country

This word was named after Vidkun Quisling (1887-1945), a Norwegian politician who gave his country to the Nazis and became a puppet ruler.

The Islamic revolutionaries felt that Arafat was a *quisling* bowing to the demands of the Israeli government, and as such, had no right to represent their interests.

RAFFISH *adj.* (RAF ish) disreputable, vulgar; characterized by a careless unconventionality, devil-may-care

This word comes from the raff of riff-raff.

He was nudged awake by a *raffish* looking fellow in search of a few pennies.

The assignation was for a deserted street in a district of *raffish* warehouses and dilapidated apartment buildings.

The party was given by a houseful of *raffish* bohemians who served spiked punch and felt no shame when putting their feet on the furniture.

RAKEHELL *n.* (RAYK hel), an evil person

This word is derived from a person so evil that he can only be found by raking hell.

Sending their kid to military school only succeeded in making him a *rakehell*, skilled only in cards and shooting guns.

RAPPROCHEMENT *n.* (ra prohsh MAH) or (RA prohsh mah) an establishment or re-establishment of good relations or harmony

The current talks in the Middle East portend a *rapprochement* between Israel and Syria.

The destruction of the Berlin wall was the most obvious symbol of the *rapprochement* between East and West Germany.

REBUS *n.* (REE buhs) a puzzle in which pictures or symbols are used to represent words

"'ICURYY4' me is a rebus for 'I see you are too wise for me.'"
—from *Webster's Unabridged Dictionary*

RECHERCHE *adj.* (rih sher SHAY) or (rih SHER shay) rare, sought out with care, choice; precious, pretentious

Ms. Maddenbody arrived with a hat that would have been *recherché* fifty years ago, but today looked merely recycled.

Despite the lurid setting and action replete with sex and violence, the author's *recherché* prose was unreadable to anyone but a true fan.

RECLAME *n* (ray KLAM) public acclaim, esp. when received through publicity; skill in publicity, showmanship

An untalented writer, Shelly Lockjaw wrote controversial articles that received great *réclame*.

The brilliant *réclame* of the liontamer served to bring him fame, fortune and an assistant to do anything at all dangerous.

RECREANT *n.* (REK ree uhnt) a coward, esp. one who gives up during a battle; a disloyal person, a traitor *adj.* unfaithful or disloyal; cowardly

The President's fortitude in sticking to his belief kept the *recreant* politicians in his own party from deserting the cause.

Although given the necessary task of teaching English to immigrants, he was *recreant* to his task, using the time to practice his Russian.

RECTITUDE *n.* (REK tuh tood) adherence to high moral standards, righteousness; correctness; straightness

Although the President's motives might have been suspect, there is no doubt of the *rectitude* of the actions undertaken.

The young sapling, bent by the gale-force winds, will regain its natural *rectitude* when the weather returns to normal.

Quick Quiz #50

Match each word in the first column with its definition in the second column. Check your answers in the back of the book.

1. quidnunc	a. tawdry
2. quisling	b. rare
3. raffish	c. acclaim
4. rakehell	d. reestablishment of relations
5. rapprochement	e. coward
6. rebus	f. rake
7. recherché	g. traitor
8. réclame	h. busybody
9. recreant	i. honesty
10. rectitude	j. picture puzzle

RECUSANT *n.* (REK yuh zuhnt) a non conformist; used in English history to refer to a Catholic who would not worship in the Church of England *adj.* refusing to conform or submit to authority; refusing to attend the Church of England

For refusing to carry a pass with their name and social security number on it, the *recusants* were given a mulct of fifty dollars.

It was considered a crime in the sixteenth century for a "popish" *recusant* to avoid the services of the Church of England.

REDOUBTABLE *adj.* (ri DOWD uhb uhl) formidable, fearsome; deserving of respect

The English, having become familiar with the longbow, became a *redoubtable* enemy, one that would pose problems for years to come.

She was pleased to be taking a class from a *redoubtable* professor who was gifted with an unusual ability to perceive the truth.

REIFY *v.* (REE uh fye) to treat (mentally) something that is abstract as if it were real

One might consider Beethoven's Ninth Symphony, for example, as beauty *reified*, i.e., it is a concrete expression of the ideal of beauty. This word is also used in political science to describe the treatment of human beings as if they were abstract forms. For example: a social security number or a SAT score are indications of the *reification* of human beings.

Marxism has a more specific sense for *reification*. It describes the alienation felt by workers who do labor for the sole purpose of receiving a paycheck. This *reification*, according to Marx, is so debilitating that it will eventually lead to a revolution.

RENASCENT *adj.* (RIH na suhnt) reborn, showing new life or vigor

The result of her fifth mugging in as many months was a *renascent* desire to return to her quiet home in Kansas.

With the dissolution of many forms of organized religion, social scientists have noticed a *renascent* paganism expressed in the so-called new-age philosophy.

REPAST *n.* (ri PAST) a meal; the act of eating

We decided to take the afternoon off from work and strolled to a nearby restaurant for a multi-course *repast*.

RESTIVE *adj.* (RES tiv) stubborn disinclination to obey orders or conform, esp. a disinclination caused by impatience or restlessness

You might wonder why a word that sounds like rest could have such contrary connotations. This word originally meant inclined to stay at rest. It reached its current meaning through first describing the actions of a horse. A restive horse is one that refuses to move when asked, and if feeling particularly ornery, moves in some perverse direction opposite to that wanted by the rider. The word is now also used to describe people who refuse to conform or follow orders.

The colonists of New England were increasingly *restive* under the regulations imposed by the king's henchmen.

RETINUE *n.* (RET uhn oo) the group of attendants who accompany a high ranking person

While the President took his morning run, a *retinue* of secret service agents were barely able to keep the pace.

The band's *retinue* had grown so large that three stretch limousines were required to transport them.

RIME *n.* (RYEM) ice formed when water freezes on grass or trees; any coating, like mud or slime, that is similar to a thin film of frost *v.* to cover with or as if covered by such ice

The schoolchildren were ensconced within the warm school bus, its windows covered with a *rime* that obscured the winter scene outside.

After two hours digging up worms in the garden, he returned to the house carrying his heavy boots which were *rimed* with mud and dead worms.

RIPOSTE *n.* (ri POHST) a quick counterthrust given after parrying an opponent's attack in fencing; a retaliatory action, a quick retort *v.* to make such a retaliatory action

The author's *riposte* upon being told that her book was hogwash was to cast doubt on the critic's sanity through a hastily written letter to the editor.

The candidate's only chance to redeem his name was a *riposte* aimed at the challenger.

ROISTER v. (ROYS tuhr) to engage in boisterous revelry; to swagger

In the wee hours of the morning, it is not unusual to find five or six rakehells *roistering* in the streets only a few feet from the liquor store.

In celebrating the completion of the final page of his vocabulary book, the author *roistered* for three days and three nights.

Quick Quiz #51

Match each word in the first column with its definition in the second column. Check your answers in the back of the book.

1. recusant		a. counterthrust
2. redoubtable		b. food
3. reify		c. reborn
4. renascent		d. coating of ice
5. repast		e. to make an abstract thing real
6. restive		f. stubborn
7. retinue		g. attendants
8. rime		h. swagger
9. riposte		i. non-conformist
10. roister		j. formidable

ROSTRUM n. (RAHS truhm) a dais or pulpit used for public speaking; the speakers' platform in an ancient Roman forum

This word comes from the Latin "rostrum" (beak) and was used in its plural form to describe the speaker's platform in ancient Rome. Adorned with the prows of ships captured from the Antiates in 338 B.C., the platforms served as stands for officials making public speeches in Rome. The word, usually used in its singular form, now refers to any raised platform used for public speaking.

The teenage Trotskyite improvised a *rostrum* out of some used crates and barrels and spoke at length of the dangers of the capitalist society.

ROUÉ n. (roo AY) or (ROO ay) a lecherous man, a rake

This word is derived from the French rouer (to break on the wheel) and was first applied to the wayward friends of the Duke of Orleans (c. 1720) who many thought should be tortured. A roué is one who deserves to be broken on the wheel.

The old *roué* played Santa at the office party to get the young women to sit on his lap.

RUBESCENT adj. (roo BES uhnt) becoming red, red

Maury's *rubescent* face was all the evidence the principal needed to prove that he was the rakehell who spilled India ink in her coffee.

RUBRIC *n.* (ROO brik) a class, concept or category; a decorative title or first letter or a book printed or underlined in red

This word from Latin "ruber" (red) was first used in English to describe the color red ochre, but was gradually used to refer to titles in book printed in red ink. The word is now most often used figuratively to represent a class, concept or category that might be "under the rubric of" a certain heading in a book.

To understand the laws that go under the *rubric* of freedom of speech, one must understand what defines speech as well as how much freedom is truly intended by the Constitution.

RUCK *n.* (RUHK) a mass, a throng, a crowd; the group of horses left behind in a race, or people who are not distinguishable as opposed to their leader

Through hard work and perseverance, Simpson was able to raise himself out of the *ruck*.

The author's living room was littered with a *ruck* of books on architecture, none of which satisfied her longing for a well-crafted romance novel.

SABULOUS *adj.* (SAB yuh luhs) sandy, gritty (also sabulose)

The wind from the *sabulous* plains left fine particles in our eyes.

SACCADIC *adj.* (sa KAD ik) relating to rapid and intermittent movement of the eye as when the eye moves from point to point while looking at different things; relating to any rapid movement, jerky

Although it might seem to you that your eyes are smoothly following this line of text, their movement could be more accurately described as *saccadic*.

Gould is one of the many theorists who believe that gradualism is not a good way to describe evolution, but that only through studying the *saccadic* movement of evolutionary development, will we understand how to explain the variety of species that have developed.

SALACIOUS *adj.* (suh LAY shuhs) lustful; stimulating sexual desire

His attitude toward the *salacious* stories was puritanical. He felt embarrassed, but continued to read them anyway.

Erma looked in the henhouse to see what the commotion was about. The *salacious* rooster had been chasing the hens again.

SALLOW *adj.* (SA loh) having a sickly greenish-yellow tone, esp. when referring to skin

Malaria had turned the missionary's pink cheeks *sallow*.

SALMAGUNDI *n.* (sal muh GUHN dee) a mixture of meat, anchovies, eggs and onions, served on lettuce; any mixture or medley

He was happy that he found the last jar of anchovies to fill his craving for *salmagundi*.

QUICK QUIZ #52

Match each word in the first column with its definition in the second column. Check your answers in the back of the book.

1. rostrum	a. medley
2. roué	b. becoming red
3. rubescent	c. lustful
4. rubric	d. mass
5. ruck	e. greenish
6. sabulous	f. rake
7. saccadic	g. sandy
8. salacious	h. pulpit
9. sallow	i. class or category
10. salmagundi	j. jerky

SANGFROID *n.* (sang FRWAH) extraordinary composure even when in danger (from French "cold blood")

 With his usual *sangfroid*, Bond tossed the grenade and walked calmly out of the room.

 Despite her apparent *sangfroid*, Leigh's legs were shaking when she walked up to the stage to accept her prize.

SAPID *adj.* (SAP id) having flavor; having a good or strong flavor; engaging

 His western tongue was not used to the mild flavors of the Buddhist monastery, but after adding a bit of soy sauce to the rice to make it *sapid*, he could stomach it.

 She was surprised at the *sapid* flavor of the game hens compared to the bland farm-raised chickens. Eating them gave her an almost unholy pleasure.

SAPIENT *adj.* (SAY pee uhnt) wise, sagacious, shrewd

 The principal's thirty years of teaching allowed him to give *sapient* advice to his pupils.

SARTORIAL *adj.* (sahr TOH ree uhl) relating to tailoring or clothing

 This word has been uttered recently by sportscasters intent on showing off their sesquipedalian vocabulary.

 The popinjay arrived at the party in his usual *sartorial* splendor, wearing a green and pink striped shirt and seersucker pants.

SASHAY *v.* (sa SHAY) to walk, to glide in an easy or casual manner; to strut; to do a certain dance move in which one foot slides sideways and is then followed by the other (like a gallop) *n.* the dance move described above; an outing

This word comes from a mistake in pronunciation or spelling of the French word "chassé" (sha SAY) which describes a square dancing move.

Four supermodels dressed to the teeth *sashayed* down the aisle to the oohs and ahs of a crowd that thought spandex was still in.

SATRAP *n.* (SAY trap) a provincial governor in ancient Persia, any governor of a larger power; one with authority; a henchman

Her request was denied by the finicky *satraps* of the state government.

SATURNINE *adj.* (SAD uhr nyen) sullen, gloomy, depressed; tending to be sarcastic

This word comes from Saturn, an ancient God who devoured his children immediately after their birth. He was forced to spit them out by his son Jupiter, who had escaped the fate of the other children. Jupiter overthrew Saturn and banished him from Olympia. The word today means gloomy, cold and comes from the astrological sense of one born under the planet's influence. A related word, saturnalia, (sad uhr NAY lyuh) comes from a festival given in Saturn's honor, and means today a period of unrestrained revelry. It seems that not all of Saturn is gloom and doom.

His *saturnine* visage was marked by a sneer that seemed to emanate from his nose to his ears.

SCABROUS *adj.* (SKA bruhs) covered with small bumps, rough, sometimes a bit slimy or scaly; full of difficulties; scandalous, lacking in delicacy, salacious, risqué

The Victorian house had not been painted in a hundred years, and the scabrous paint made the new owners of the home a little nervous.

With her car out of gas three hundred miles from civilization, Delilah realized that she was in a *scabrous* situation. She had nothing to do but to begin trudging back.

A man at the door was hawking *scabrous* scandal sheets that had a certain famous rock star's name all over them.

SCALAWAG *n.* (SKAL ih wag) someone disreputable, a reprobate, a scamp; a Southern white person who accepted the laws of the reconstruction (also scalawag, scallywag, scallawag, and skalawag)

"Why is it," she wondered, "that the only dates I have are with the worst *scalawags* to ever make eyes at a woman."

The Southern town was descended upon by a cadre of mountebanks, carpet-baggers, and *scalawags* who proceeded to steal or con the poor unsuspecting ingénues out of the last of their money.

SCHADENFREUDE *n.* (SHAH duhn froy duh) guilty pleasure one feels when others are suffering

Several English lexicographers (who must have felt some animosity to Germany) have taken immense pleasure in the fact that a word to describe this particular feeling exists only in German.

Having walked in during a lull, Mica was not completely without *schadenfreude* at witnessing the long line forming behind her at the door.

QUICK QUIZ #53

Match each word in the first column with its definition in the second column. Check your answers in the back of the book.

1. sangfroid	a. related to clothing
2. sapid	b. rough
3. sapient	c. composed
4. sartorial	d. shrewd
5. sashay	e. tasty
6. satrap	f. to glide
7. saturnine	g. pleasure in suffering
8. scabrous	h. governor
9. scalawag	i. gloomy
10. schadenfreude	j. scamp

SCHLEMIEL *n.* (shluh MEEL) a foolish, unlucky, clumsy wimp (also schlemihl or shlemiel) (from Yiddish)

A *schlemiel* is usually treated with scorn and not pity.

SCHLIMAZEL *n.* (shlih MAH zuhl) a "born loser," an unlucky simp (also schlimazl or shlimazel or shlimazl) (from Yiddish)

A schlimazel, although similar to a schlemiel, is slightly different. While both are unlucky, the schlemiel is more likely to be the cause of his own misfortune.

If a banana peel were lying dangerously on the street, a schlemiel would slip on it. But if that schlemiel happened to be carrying a heavy suitcase, and in the process of slipping, he tossed the suitcase up in the air and it fell on someone, the person hit by the suitcase would be called a *schlimazel*.

SCINTILLA *n.* (sin TIL uh) an iota, a small amount; a spark

She entered the room and headed directly to the buffet table, moving without a *scintilla* of grace.

The least *scintilla* of hope is often enough for a Panglossian optimist to dance for joy.

SCION *n.* (SYE uhn) an offshoot of a plant, a twig; an heir

Without much hope, the young gardeners stuck a *scion* from an oak tree in good soil, and were surprised to see it grow in several years into a sturdy sapling.

Vice President Duck, the wealthy *scion* of an industrial magnate, repeated often the ludicrous assertion that he was a self-made man.

SCOFFLAW *n.* (SKAHF law) one who is continually breaking the law

This word was coined in a 1929 contest in Boston to find the best word to describe a "lawless drinker." The winners, Henry Irving Dale and Miss Kate L. Butler, each were awarded $100 for their suggestion, which was picked out of 25,000 others. The word is now used to describe one who continually breaks the law, especially if it is one who refuses to pay parking tickets.

Neighboring states have been cooperating lately to capture *scofflaws* who routinely park illegally but feel that they are immune because their cars are registered somewhere else.

SCREED *n.* (SKREED) a long and monotonous tirade or a long letter

My hands were shaking after reading Egbert's *screed* of malevolence sent in response to my innocent request.

My sister would send a *screed* from time to time to tell me how she was doing.

SEDULOUS *adj.* (SEH juh luhs) assiduous, industrious, painstaking

Only through *sedulous* analysis, was the lab assistant able to discover the secret to Superman's power.

SEMIOTICS *n.* (see mye AHD iks) or (seh mee AHD iks) semantics

Semiotics is the study of signs and what is signified by the signs. First developed by Charles Sanders Peirce (1839–1914), it has been used as a tool for studying language, gesture, and visual imagery. The tools of semiotics are used in other fields including sociology, anthropology, and philosophy.

For her senior thesis, Elaine did a *semiotic* analysis of the advertising media used to sell breakfast cereal.

SEPTUM *n.* (SEP tuhm) a thin dividing wall that separates two cavities or areas of soft tissue in an organism

Using certain types of illegal drugs has been shown to damage the nasal *septum*. Habitual cocaine users have noses with only one nostril.

SEQUACIOUS *adj.* (sih KWAY shuhs) tending to follow, slavish, obsequious; following logically

Fear of the other has tended to help demagogues control the *sequacious* herd of self-proclaimed "free thinking" individuals.

The workings of his mind, while somewhat slow, were *sequacious*; subsequently, he always arrived at the answer.

QUICK QUIZ #54

Match each word in the first column with its definition in the second column. Check your answers in the back of the book.

1. schlemiel	a. semantics
2. schlimazel	b. unlucky simp
3. scintilla	c. unlucky fool
4. scion	d. a tiny bit
5. scofflaw	e. tirade
6. screed	f. a continual lawbreaker
7. sedulous	g. biological partition
8. semiotics	h. slavish
9. septum	i. an heir
10. sequacious	j. painstaking

SERE *adj.* (SIUHR) dry, withered (also sear)

The sound of *sere* leaves crepitating accompanied their every step.

The drought left behind a sabulous plain with islands of *sere* vegetation and a few emaciated prairie dogs looking for food.

SERIF *n.* (SER if) those little lines that are used in printing on the end of broad strokes used to form the lines of a letter

This text is set in a font with *serifs*. Notice the fine lines on the ends of the stroke that makes the "s."

SESQUIPEDALIAN *n.* (ses kwih pih DAY lyuhn) a long word, or one with many syllables *adj.* given to using long words

This word comes from the Latin "sesquipedalis" (a foot and a half long) and was used by Horace in A.D. 97 to describe a list of long words in Latin.

The editor's job was made more onerous by the first-time author's turgid style and love of *sesquipedalian* words.

His love of *sesquipedalians* was beginning to annoy his girlfriend, who felt that his time would be better spent getting a job than learning another polysyllabic way of saying sand.

SESSILE *adj.* (SE suhl) or (SE syel) sedentary, not free to move

Having finished a long week of twelve-hour days, he knew that he wanted to spend the next few hours in a *sessile* state with his eyes glued to the television.

Because they do not need to avoid objects, most *sessile* animals do not have the ability to see.

SIBILANT *adj.* (SIB uh luhnt) characterized by the hiss that one makes when making the "s" sound *n.* a sibilant sound

The search party halted abruptly when it heard the *sibilant* snake.

All languages have some type of *sibilant* consonant.

SIMULACRUM *n.* (sim yuh LAY kruhm) an image; a vague representation or semblance

The soap star, who had been dragged to the London Wax works museum, was disturbed to see her *simulacrum* standing in front of her, mouth agape with eyes that never blinked.

To fool the German army, the British army set up a *simulacrum* of its tanks and artillery that led the Germans to believe that the attack was to come somewhere else.

SINE QUA NON *n.* (si nay kwah NOHN) or (si nay kwah NAHN) something that is an essential condition or element

This phrase comes from Latin "sine qua non" (without which not).

The maraschino cherry on top, no matter how vile tasting, is the *sine qua non* of an ice cream sundae.

SINECURE *n.* (SYE nih kyoor) or (SIN uh kyoor) a job or position that pays a salary but requires no work

Becoming an elected official gave the city councilor the power to hand out *sinecures* to all her friends.

Author Eliot was hoping to quit her job sweeping the streets so that she could find some *sinecure* to pay the bills while she concentrated on her novel.

SISYPHEAN *adj.* (sis uh FEE uhn) requiring a continual and ineffective effort

This word comes from the Greek myth in which King Sisyphus was punished by the gods for his reluctance to be put in hell. Through some clever maneuvering, Sisyphus had been able to escape from Tartarus, a place of mortal punishment, two times. When he was finally caught and dragged down into the infernal realm, he was forced to push a heavy rock up a hill. Whenever the rock came near the top, some unknown force would push it to the bottom again, and poor Sisyphus, sweating from his exertion, would run down to the bottom of the hill and push it up again. A Sisyphean labor is one that, like Sisyphus's efforts to push the rock up the hill, is never-ending and futile.

Congress's attempt to balance the budget was a *Sisyphean* task. When a bill with a balanced budget was brought to committee, it was returned with the requirement that taxes be cut, at which point it was forced back to the committee.

SLATTERNLY *adj.* (SLAD uhrn lee) squalid, unkempt or dirty because of neglect; characteristic of a prostitute

It was hard to believe just how completely such a *slatternly* woman, dressed in rags, could be transformed through a bath and a trip to Bloomingdales.

The walls of the *slatternly* apartment were covered from floor to ceiling with posters of obsolete movies of the sixties.

Quick Quiz #55

Match each word in the first column with its definition in the second column. Check your answers in the back of the book.

1. sere	a. fine lines on letters
2. serif	b. image
3. sesquipedalian	c. long word
4. sessile	d. dry
5. sibilant	e. sedentary
6. simulacrum	f. squalid
7. sine qua non	g. easy job
8. sinecure	h. needing continual effort
9. Sisyphean	i. the "s" sound
10. slatternly	j. something essential

SMARMY *adj.* (SMAHR mee) hypocritically earnest; unctuous

She knew she shouldn't have accepted the *smarmy* swine's offer to sashay together out to Seattle, but something about his clear blue eyes convinced her.

SNOLLYGOSTER *n.* (SNAHL lee gahs tuhr) a politician who is concerned not with consistent principles, but rather with looking out for his own interests (slang)

Some lexicographers believe that this word is related to the word "snallygaster", a creature of the mythology of rural Maryland that was believed to eat small children and poultry. President Harry Truman was fond of snollygoster and used it a few times in speeches.

Unless some type of campaign finance reform is undertaken, the House will be controlled by a group of *snollygosters* who will pay no heed to the needs of the people.

SOBRIQUET *n.* (SOH bruh kay) a nickname, usually humorous or affectionate; an assumed name

This word is from Celtic origin, and means literally "a chuck under the chin."

Some famous *sobriquets* of Presidents are "Rough Rider" for Teddy Roosevelt, "Give 'Em Hell Harry" for Harry S. Truman, and "Silent Cal" for Calvin Coolidge.

SOLECISM *n.* (SAH luh siz uhm) or (SOH luh siz uhm) a violation of grammatical rules; a breach of etiquette; something improper, abnormal, or illogical

The manuscript was so full of *solecisms* that it would be easier to rewrite it from scratch than to edit it.

The *solecism* in this sentence were made intentionally.

SOLIPSISM *n.* (SOH lip siz uhm) or (SAH lip siz uhm) a theory in philosophy that only the self can be known to exist; extreme focus on the self as opposed to relationships with others

A *solipsist* believes that anything outside of her own personal experience is only a figment of consciousness.

Her poetry suffered from *solipsism*; it had no references to anything other than herself.

SOMNAMBULIST *n.* (sahm NAM byuh list) a sleepwalker

It's not a good idea to wake a *somnambulist*, especially if she is standing on a cliff.

SOUGH *v.* (SAOW) or (SUHF) to make a murmuring or sighing sound *n.* a soft murmuring sound

The ocean winds *soughed* through the branches of the sycamore tree on a hot summer day.

For the first time in twenty years she fell asleep serenaded by the *sough* of the surf.

SOUPÇON *n.* (soop SOHn) a tiny bit, a trace, a hint, a suspicion

A *soupçon* of anger could be detected in his voice as he told his daughter for the fiftieth time that no, he had not taken her baseball glove.

As she graded the student's exams, the teacher realized that there was not a *soupçon* of sense in any of them.

SPECIE *n.* (SPEE shee) coin, as in money

This word is also used in an idiom "in specie," which either means in kind or in coin.

After the government is destroyed, currency will have no value, but *specie* will still be worth the metal it is coined in.

She felt that to repay his cruelties in *specie* was the only appropriate act.

SPELUNKER *n.* (spih LUHNG kuhr) one whose hobby is to explore caves

An avid *spelunker*, Zweibel was able to crawl through the smallest tunnels.

On their first date, he took his future wife *spelunking* in Howe caverns where they got lost and ended up travelling two days without food.

QUICK QUIZ #56

Match each word in the first column with its definition in the second column. Check your answers in the back of the book.

1. smarmy		a.	nickname
2. snollygoster		b.	a tiny bit
3. sobriquet		c.	violation of grammar
4. solecism		d.	cave explorer
5. solipsism		e.	soft sighing noise
6. somnambulist		f.	coin
7. sough		g.	sleepwalker
8. soupçon		h.	an unprincipled politician
9. specie		i.	unctuous
10. spelunker		j.	focus on self

SPHYGMOMANOMETER *n.* (sfig MOH mah nawm uhd uhr) an instrument used to measure blood pressure We have to admit that we only included this word because it is so much fun to say.

Using a *sphygmomanometer*, the nurse determined that my blood pressure was too high and he ordered me to get some exercise.

SPLENETIC *adj.* (splih NED ik) related to the spleen; showing ill humor or irritability *n.* an irritable person

A splenetic is one who is quick to anger and at the same time morose, vindictive, and generally nasty. Much as the heart today is thought to symbolize the seat of love and other emotions, the spleen, an organ known today to regulate the blood, was thought in the Middle Ages to be both the seat of violent emotions and of laughter.

Hoping for a positive review, the author opened the pages of Kirkus with eager anticipation. Unfortunately, the article was *splenetic* in tone, casting his book as one of the worst ever written.

The *splenetic* behind the counter refused to return his change and instead spit in his face.

SPOONERISM *n.* (SPOON uh riz uhm) a transposition of the consonant sounds in two words, esp. if the resulting words have some sort of comic effect

This word is named after Archibald Spooner (1844–1930), a dean of New College, Oxford who was often uttering some spoonerism or other, like, for example: "For pure enjoyment, give me a well-boiled icycle."

STENTORIAN *adj.* (sten TOH ree uhn) extremely loud

This word comes from Stentor, a warrior mentioned in the Iliad "whose voice was as powerful as fifty voices of other men," and it is usually used in discussing voices. A stentorian voice is one that has great power, range and resonance.

His wife used her *stentorian* voice to remind him that they were late for their appointment, and she succeeded in waking the entire block.

The child, usually shy, found herself in possession of a microphone, and in a painfully *stentorian* tone, announced that she was ready to go home.

STRAPPADO *n.* (struh PAY doh) or (struh PAH doh) a torture in which a person has his hands tied behind his back and is lifted and then dropped with all the weight on the tied hands

Strappado, used during the inquisition, seems to be something to avoid if at all possible.

STRIATED *n.* (strye AYD uhd) marked with lines or ridges

The bark that had appeared smooth from a distance appeared finely *striated* under a microscope.

The *striated* crystal produced a beautiful pattern when held up to the light.

Scientists still debate the purpose of the *striae* found on many shells.

STRUCTURALISM *n.* (STRUHK chuhr uh liz uhm) a method of analyzing phenomena in which the phenomena is broken down into its most stable and elemental structures

Structuralism, the study of the underlying structures and patterns and their interrelationships, is used in linguistics, anthropology, psychology, and literature. In linguistics, it involves the separation of form and substance. In the social sciences, it concerns the underlying interrelationships between social structures.

At one time, *structuralists* believed that our ability to perceive colors was determined by our linguistic capacity to name them.

STURM UND DRANG *n.* (shtoor moont DRAHNG) turmoil; a late eighteenth century German literary movement in which a person's individual struggle against conventional society was a typical theme

The word, which comes from the German Sturm und Drang (storm and stress), was the title of a drama by Friedrich Maximilian von Klinger, and was used to describe an eighteenth century literary movement which often depicted a stormy individual who struggled against the injustices of conventional society. The word is also used to mean storm and stress or turmoil.

She would have been more comfortable living in that time of *Sturm and Drang*, when to scream poetry from the side of a mountain was a romantic ideal.

The *Sturm und Drang* of life was getting to be more than Michiko could handle. She needed quiet, and decided that it was time to head for the country.

STYGIAN *adj.* (STIJ ee uhn) relating to the river Styx; gloomy, dark; hellish; unbreakable (oath)

This word refers to the Styx, the river which must be crossed for a soul to enter the underworld. As you might imagine, this gateway to hell was cold and dark and possessed strange powers. Achilles, the great warrior of the Iliad, was dipped here by his mother to protect him, but because she held him by his heel, that area of his anatomy was not protected. The word is also used to refer to an inviolable oath. Just as we used to swear on a bible to prove our truthfulness, the gods would swear on some water from the river Styx.

The blackout threw the city into a *stygian* darkness where the few people with flashlights held all the power.

The President took a *stygian* oath to reduce the deficit and lower taxes, but no one believed him anyway.

SUB-ROSA *adj.* (suh BROH zuh) secret, confidential (sub-rosa) *adv.* secretly, confidentially (sub rosa)

This word which means in Latin literally "under the rose" got its meaning from the ancient practice of hanging a flower over banquet tables during the middle ages. In Roman mythology, Harpocrates, the god of silence, was given a rose by Cupid in exchange for keeping mum after having stumbled upon Venus, Cupid's mother, in an illicit affair.

The leaking of the *sub-rosa* report on the imminent danger of nuclear war to the press caused panic in the streets.

The committee met *sub rosa* and discussed terms for starting the impeachment process.

QUICK QUIZ #57

Match each word in the first column with its definition in the second column. Check your answers in the back of the book.

1. sphygmomanometer	a. irritable
2. splenetic	b. dark
3. spoonerism	c. turmoil
4. stentorian	d. blood pressure measurer
5. strappado	e. secret
6. striated	f. loud
7. structuralism	g. lined
8. Sturm und Drang	h. breaking down of phenomenon
9. stygian	i. torture
10. sub-rosa	j. transposing of letters in words

SUCCUBUS *n.* (SUHK yuh buhs) a female demon who was supposed to have sexual intercourse with sleeping men; a demon or fiend; a prostitute

The succubus and its male counterpart the incubus (ING kyuh buhs) (who seduced women), seem a bit silly today, but these creatures were taken very seriously in the Middle Ages where they were recognized by civil and church law.

The only way to explain Murphy's gleeful expression at breakfast is that he was visited by a *succubus* last night.

SUI GENERIS *adj.* (soo eye JEH nuhr is) unique, of its own kind

This word is sometimes used after the noun it modifies.

Although plainly derivative of other books of its kind, the mystery novel did have some *sui generis* qualities.

The audience sat transfixed listening to Beethoven's incredible symphony *sui generis.*

SUI JURIS *adj.* (soo eye JOO ris) competent to manage one's own affairs (law)

When she turned eighteen and became *sui juris,* her first act was to quit school and hitchhike across the country.

SULLY *v.* (suh LEE) to dirty, soil or stain; to defile

Anita Hunt's accusations had somewhat *sullied* his name, but he became a Supreme Court justice, nevertheless.

The dust from the road *sullied* his newly purchased white t-shirt.

SUPERNAL *adj.* (soo PUHRN uhl) from above; from heaven

This word is the opposite of infernal.

The sea parted and Maxwell awaited some *supernal* communication from whatever agent had caused such a miracle.

The *supernal* melodies of the Gregorian chant blared from his sound system, causing the walls to resonate as if he were in a cathedral.

SUSURRATE *v.* (suh SUH rayt) to make a soft rustling sound, to whisper *n.* a whispering sound

The room had an eerie quiet only broken by the soft classical music *susurrating* from the balcony.

As the couple settled down to sleep, they heard a *susurrus* of chatter from the apartment next door.

SVELTE *adj.* (SFELT) or (SVELT) slender, thin; elegant, sophisticated

A hush filled the room as eleven *svelte* supermodels glided by.

Their home had no reading material other than a *svelte* newspaper full of urbane stories of the upper class.

SYBARITIC *adj* (sib uh RID ik) hedonistic; of or related to a native of Sybaris

This word comes from the ancient Sybarites who were known for their luxurious, soft effeminate lifestyle. It implies an extreme sensuousness or voluptuousness, an overrefined sensibility and enjoyment of rare food.

The seventh course of this *Sybaritic* banquet was so good that those that partook could only sigh with glee before falling asleep.

After winning the lottery, the formerly industrious laborer took for himself a life of *Sybaritic* elegance.

SYLLOGISM *n.* (SIL uh jiz uhm) a form of logic in which major and minor premises are made, and from them a conclusion is drawn; the process of deduction; a crafty or specious argument

The following is an example of a syllogism:

Major Premise: All people reading this book are brilliant. Minor Premise: You are reading this book. Conclusion: You are a brilliant.

His belief in the absurd *syllogism*, all's well that ends well, will cost him his job.

SYLVAN *adj.* (SIL vuhn) like the woods; inhabiting a forest; wooded, with many trees (also silvan)

The north wood's *sylvan* silence, so loved by naturalists, is broken every five minutes by the roar of an airplane.

We entered the outdoor cafe along a *sylvan* path that belied our location in the center of the world's largest city.

QUICK QUIZ #58

Match each word in the first column with its definition in the second column. Check your answers in the back of the book.

1. succubus	a. whisper
2. sui generis	b. legally competent
3. sui juris	c. from heaven
4. sully	d. wood like
5. supernal	e. demon who sleeps with men
6. susurrate	f. dirty
7. svelte	g. thin
8. Sybaritic	h. hedonistic
9. syllogism	i. deductive reasoning
10. sylvan	j. unique

SYNCRETISM *n.* (SING kruh tiz uhm) a fusion of differing systems of belief or philosophy

This word was used specifically to describe a seventeenth century attempt by George Calixtus to reconcile the Lutheran church with the Protestant and the Catholic, and is now used in a somewhat derogatory fashion.

No one was pleased by the poorly conceived *syncretism* of Catholic and Buddhist religions.

SYNECDOCHE *n.* (sih NEK duh kee) a rhetorical device in which a part is used to represent the whole; a figure of speech in which the more comprehensive is used to represent the less comprehensive

The following are examples of *synecdoche*:
The farmhand picked the vegetables. He was pulled over by the law. He attacked, flinging his steel at him in a graceful arc.

SYNERGY *n.* (SIH nuhr jee) when combined or cooperative force is stronger than its individual parts (also synergism)

His talent for melody and hers for songwriting resulted in a wonderful *synergy* that produced some of the best musicals ever written.

When the maker of dog toys bought the manufacturer of dog food, they aimed to create a *synergy* that would produce more sales.

SYNESTHESIA *n.* (sin ihs THEEZH uh) when one sense informs the other (a sound makes one see color); a description of one sense with a term used in another sense (loud pattern) (also synaesthesia) For example: The violinist's loud shirt could not compete with the sweet sounds of the concerto.

Stravinsky's music is effective at producing a *synesthesia* in many listeners who see colors when exposed to his music.

TARANTISM *n.* (TAR uhn tiz uhm) a disorder in which the victim has an uncontrollable urge to dance, esp. in Italy in the fifteenth to seventeenth centuries.

It was thought that this urge to dance was caused by the bite of a tarantula.
P-funk came on loud at the club and bodies began to shake and shimmy as if infected with *tarantism*.

TATTERDEMALION *n.* (tad uhr dih MAY lyuhn) one wearing rags or tattered clothes *adj.* ragged

In her attempts to get home quickly to her tony apartment, she nearly stumbled over a filthy *tatterdemalion* living above a grate on Fifth Avenue.

A gorgeous quilt, constructed of *tatterdemalion* scraps, was presented to the first person to guess the number of ping-pong balls in a large jar.

TAWDRY *adj.* (TAW dree) gaudy, showy in poor taste

This word comes from tawdry lace, a bit of lace worn around a woman's neck for decoration. Such a decoration was considered cheap and gaudy. Tawdry lace, in turn, is a contraction of St. Audrey, a seventh century queen of Norway who died of a tumor in her neck that was said to have been caused by her love of necklaces. A festival was given every year in her honor at which cheap and tawdry necklaces could be bought.

The *tawdry* language used in her new novel did not impress anyone.

TECTONIC *adj.* (tek TAH nik) having to do with structural changes in the earth's crust; architectural, related to construction

The mountainous island of Hawaii seems to have been created through *tectonic* activity.

The greatest American practitioner of the *tectonic* arts is no doubt Frank Lloyd Wright.

TELEOLOGY *n.* (tel EE ahl uh jee) philosophical inquiry into purpose of natural phenomena; explaining a phenomenon by its end or purpose

An example of a teleological theory is Lamark's theories of evolution. Lamark held that over generations, a giraffe might stretch its neck to reach a higher branch. Each generation's neck would get longer, producing the giraffe we see today. Because the argument is made by looking at the end result and extrapolating backwards, it is teleological.

TENDENTIOUS *adj.* (ten DEN chuhs) partisan, having or advancing a definite point of view, biased

He had no choice but to argue that such a *tendentious* assertion would add nothing to the search for the truth.

Many feel that the Halloween legends of ghouls and goblins were *tendentious*, invented to provide parents with a way of scaring their young children into staying close to home.

QUICK QUIZ #59

Match each word in the first column with its definition in the second column. Check your answers in the back of the book.

1.	syncretism	a.	figure of speech
2.	synecdoche	b.	fusion of philosophy
3.	synergy	c.	one sense informs the other
4.	synesthesia	d.	ragged
5.	tarantism	e.	relating to Earth's crust
6.	tatterdemalion	f.	combined forces stronger than individual
7.	tawdry	g.	gaudy
8.	tectonic	h.	dance crazy
9.	teleology	i.	partisan
10.	tendentious	j.	study of purpose

TENEBROUS *adj.* (TEN uh bruhs) gloomy, dark

When the trap door was opened, light seared into the *tenebrous* oubliette, and the temporarily blinded prisoners were unable to escape.

The *tenebrous* novel was geared to attract readers who were as fond of goblins as of romance.

TERGIVERSATE *v.* (TER jih ver sayt) to equivocate, evade, esp. in a dishonorable manner; to desert a cause; apostatize

After four hours during which he wavered and *tergiversated*, he finally admitted that he had, in fact, killed his brother.

He had been noble to the cause for years, but upon meeting a cute member of the Young Republican's club, he *tergiversated*, and admitted that maybe labor unions weren't so great after all.

The President was accused of duplicity and *tergiversation* for his evasive answers concerning his draft-dodging during the sixties.

TERMAGANT *n.* (TUHR muh guhnt) a quarrelsome women, a shrew, a nag

He would comfort his jealous second wife by telling stories of his first, a bullying *termagant* who enjoyed making him look stupid in front of his friends.

THAUMATURGY *n* (THAW muh tuhr jee) the performance of miracles or magic

The island natives looked at the coke bottle as if it were a product of some type of mystical *thaumaturgy*.

Many religious thinkers view Jesus's *thaumaturgy* as metaphor rather than as actual happenings.

THEODICY *n.* (thee AH duh see) a vindication of God's benevolence despite the existence of evil

Used as the title of a work by Leibniz (1710), in which he discussed God and the existence of evil, theodicy is an optimistic attempt to justify evil in the world, and to show that it is all part of the master plan.

She developed her *theodicy* after the death of her husband and their young son. She believed that some good had to come out of such a tragedy.

THEOSOPHY *n.* (thee AH suh fee) any religion that believes that the nature of the soul can be discovered through mystical insight, i.e., meditation; the beliefs of the Theosophical society, established in New York City (1875), which incorporated aspects of Buddhism

As the rector aged, his literal interpretation of the Bible degenerated into an abstruse *theosophy* that could only be understood through meditation and hallucinogenic drugs.

THRALL *n.* (THRAWL) a slave or serf; one who is psychologically a slave; bondage

Through the effective use of her wiles she was able to hold him in *thrall* for over two years before he realized that she was just stringing him along.

We, as a nation, have become a people in *thrall* to the advantages of a free market economy.

THRENODY *n.* (THREH noh dee) a poem or song of mourning, a dirge

The mourners were greatly moved by the recitation of a *threnody* composed by W. H. Auden.

THROTTLEBOTTOM *n.* (THRAHD uhl bah tuhm) a useless vice president

This word comes from the 1931 Satire "Of Thee I sing," where Vice President Throttlebottom needed a guided tour to see the White House.

The current Vice President can be held in stark contrast to the *Throttlebottom* who preceded him.

TINCTURE *n.* (TING chuhr) a tiny bit of something, a hint
v. to dye; to infuse with some characteristic

Although obviously self-serving, his lickspittle flattery appeared to its recipient as having a *tincture* of sincerity.

The fountain had been *tinctured* with some awful pea-green dye that made the water look diseased.

The great raconteur *tinctured* his sentences with his warm personality, giving great pleasure to any who would listen.

Quick Quiz #60

Match each word in the first column with its definition in the second column. Check your answers in the back of the book.

1.	tenebrous	a.	dirge
2.	tergiversate	b.	belief in meditation
3.	termagant	c.	performing miracles
4.	thaumaturgy	d.	God really is good
5.	theodicy	e.	bad vice-president
6.	theosophy	f.	a hint
7.	thrall	g.	dark
8.	threnody	h.	equivocate
9.	throttlebottom	i.	slave
10.	tincture	j.	shrew

TINTINNABULATION *n.* (tin tuh na byuh LAY shuhn) the sound made when bells ring

His home, surrounded on four sides by churches, was shaken every hour by the *tintinnabulation* of ten church bells.

TITIVATE *v.* (TID uh vayt) to decorate, spruce up, make alterations in one's appearance

This word is sometimes used as an incorrect substitution for titillate.

She spent the final moments before her date *titivating* herself in front of the mirror.

In the second or so before she turned around, the coxcomb surreptitiously *titivated* his hair and checked himself in the rearview mirror.

TOADY *n.* (TOH dee) a sycophant, one who flatters someone for his own purposes *v.* to fawn or act in a servile manner

This word, as you might expect, comes from toad, and it used to describe a little toad. But you might wonder how a little toad could be considered a bootlicker. It seems that certain mountebanks worked a confidence game claiming they could cure poison. A charlatan would have an assistant eat toads, which were considered extremely poisonous, and then miraculously cure him. Obviously someone who would eat a toad would do almost anything, and the word "toadeater" became synonymous with this type of servile behavior. Eventually, this word influenced its current meaning.

Misty was a typical bureaucrat, a *toady* to her superiors, and a bully to anyone working under her.

Dave Nixon *toadied* to his boss one too many times. His coworkers retaliated by stealing all his Post-It notes.

TOME *n.* (TOHM) a book, esp. a large, heavy scholarly book

The stingy man pulled a huge thirty-five-pound *tome* of the top shelf and let it drop onto the floor with a thud. "I will never need to buy another book" he thought to himself.

In seeking the answer to life's most ponderous question, he waded through numerous *tomes*, but presently gave up and moved to Rio.

TONY *adj.* (TOH nee) aristocratic, hoity-toity, fashionable, having a high tone (also toney)

This word derives from tone and a secondary meaning of the word "ton" (TOHN) which can mean fashion or hipness.

A week after crawling through the mud-slung hills of Vietnam, he found himself in the *tony* atmosphere of the Tokyo Hilton, wearing a tuxedo and diamond cuff-links.

Every German town has one place where the *tony* women go to have tea.

TOOTHSOME *adj.* (TOOTH suhm) tasty; pleasant; sexually attractive, luscious

Even in the hands of a seasoned chef, who would have thought roast duck could be so *toothsome*? Tender and moist, the meat practically fell off the bones.

The revolutionaries who gained control of the state house in a successful putsch found their first taste of power *toothsome*. The process of governing however, proved a bit of a bore, and they quickly tired of it.

TOR *n.* (TAWR) a high rocky hill or pile of rocks

With one leg broken and without food atop a lonely *tor*, the rock climber was ecstatic when a lumbering St. Bernard found him and barked loudly to alert his master of the climber's whereabouts.

TRADE-LAST *n.* (TRAYD last) a compliment that one has overheard and is willing to trade to a person if that person will repeat a favorable remark made about oneself (informal)

In return for passing on Romeo's thoughts to Juliet, Mercutio received a *trade-last* in return.

TRICE *n.* (TRYES) an instant, a short period of time

This word used to mean a yank, as in to yank up a sail, and the phrase "in one trice" meant quickly. The current meaning is derived from this sense.

"I'll be back in a *trice*," she said as she got into her car. But they both knew that she was off to Las Vegas to become a Huey Newton groupie.

TROGLODYTE *n.* (TRAHG luh dyet) a member of any ancient or mythological race that dwelt in caves; a recluse, a brutish person, a hermit

Early man is mistakenly assumed to be a *troglodyte*, but evidence shows he spent most of his time in trees.

Although he might seem to be modern in his ways, his outmoded political beliefs made him a *troglodyte*.

QUICK QUIZ #61

Match each word in the first column with its definition in the second column. Check your answers in the back of the book.

1. tintinnabulation		a.	bell noise
2. titivate		b.	caveman
3. toady		c.	sycophant
4. tome		d.	purchased complement
5. tony		e.	rocky crag
6. toothsome		f.	aristocratic
7. tor		g.	decorate
8. trade-last		h.	a short time
9. trice		i.	tasty
10. troglodyte		j.	big book

TROPE *n.* (TROHP) the use of a word in a figurative sense, a figure of speech

A trope is the use of a word in a non-literal sense. Examples include metaphors, similes, synecdoche, and metonymy.

The extensive *tropes* used in Eliot's "Wasteland" give the poem its expressive power and also make it such a challenge to understand.

TRUCKLE *n.* (TRUH kuhl) a small wheel used to make it easier to move heavy furniture, a caster *v.* to be subservient or servile

While you might think that the two modern meanings of this word are unrelated, if looked at historically they make sense. A *truckle*, in the fifteenth century, was a pulley used to lift things, and it was only a small step from this to its current meaning of a caster. These casters were used in what later became known as a truckle bed, where one bed slides out from underneath the other on truckles. A person sleeping on the lower bunk was said to truckle under the person sleeping on the top bunk. From this meaning, it was only a short step to the current meaning of subservient. One who "*truckles under*" would, of course, be taking the inferior position.

Those who had been the most outspoken in their criticism of the President were also the ones most apt to *truckle* down to him when they needed to ask a favor.

TRUCULENT *adj.* (TRUHK yuh luhnt) ready to fight, pugnacious; fierce, cruel; deadly; scathing

The invention of such a *truculent* bomb, while a scientific achievement, was sure to increase tensions between the superpowers.

This *truculent* document, quietly shifted from publisher to publisher, finally exploded onto the public stage when its most scathing accusations were leaked to the press.

TUMESCENCE *n.* (too MES uhns) a swelling; swelling fullness

The slight *tumescence* of Mount St. Helens, although worrisome, is not an indication of an immediate eruption.

The music had an expressive quality that led to a *tumescence* of the spirit, a love of life.

TURGID *adj.* (TUHR jid) grandiloquent, excessively complicated style in language, bombastic; swollen

Why any professor would assign such a verbose and *turgid* tome to twenty-two-year-olds is a complete mystery.

Maple trees in the spring have trunks *turgid* with sap, waiting to be tapped to make syrup.

TWIT *v.* (TWIT) to tease, ridicule in a good humored way; *n.* the act of ridiculing; a taunt; *slang* a fool

Some of the other plumbers *twitted* him for his high-brow tastes, calling him a toilet don.

Even years after the event, her husband would give an occasional *twit* at her for her infantile behavior at the awards ceremony.

TYRO *n.* (TYE roh) a beginner, one who understands the basics but lacks any experience (also tiro)

The merest *tyro* in music can tell when a chord clashes or a note is out of place.

A *tyro* in the sport of golf, Maxwell had only the vaguest ideas about which club to use.

UBIETY *n.* (YOO bye uhd ee) the quality of being in a particular position or location, whereness

The novel's lack of *ubiety* gave it a universality that would have been difficult to achieve had the setting been in a particular community or country.

ULULATE *v.* (UHL yuh layt) or (YOOL yuh layt) to wail or howl loudly

The howling of a wolf, a fixture of early prairie life once has been replaced by the *ululating* of sirens in the city.

The stands shook with the ecstatic *ululation* of the crowd when the home team won.

UMBRAGE n. (UHM brij) displeasure or resentment; something providing shade or shade; a hint

A nebbish by nature, Nick knew that to take *umbrage* for such a slight would lead to a confrontation.

The couple gave *umbrage* to many of their friends by giving a small wedding and only inviting family.

The fishermen emerged from the *umbrage* of the deep woods into the sunny clearing and its trout-filled stream.

QUICK QUIZ #62

Match each word in the first column with its definition in the second column. Check your answers in the back of the book.

1. trope	a. displeasure
2. truckle	b. swelling
3. truculent	c. figure of speech
4. tumescence	d. beginner
5. turgid	e. ridicule
6. twit	f. pugnacious
7. tyro	g. whereness
8. ubiety	h. be servile
9. ululate	i. grandiloquent
10. umbrage	j. howl

UNDULATE v. (UHN juh layt) to move smoothly in a wavelike motion; to cause to move smoothly in a wavelike motion

The performance featured a dozen exotic dancers *undulating* their bellies in rhythm to loud rap music.

In contrast to the rough seas of the recently departed storm, today's waves *undulated* restfully.

UXORIOUS adj. (uhk SOH ree uhs) excessively submissive or fond of one's wife

Having strong *uxorious* tendencies, Samuel spent his free time bragging about how lucky he was to have such a great wife.

VAINGLORIOUS adj. (vayn GLOHR ee uhs) boastful, pompous

His pretentious and *vainglorious* air kept anyone with a shred of self-worth from becoming his friend.

The uxorious husband, *vainglorious* of his wife's charms, spent every waking moment talking about her.

VALETUDINARIAN *n.* (val uh tood uhn ER ee uhn) an unhealthy person, esp. one who is obsessed with his health; *adj.* sickly, infirm; being obsessed with one's health

A self-absorbed *valetudinarian*, Nixon did not put anything in his mouth until he knew whether it had been properly cleaned.

He had the *valetudinarian* habit of staying inside during the rainy season.

VASSAL *n.* (VA suhl) a person who in return for his obedience, took care of the land of and received protection from a feudal lord; a slave; a subordinate

As China's power has increased, the nations on its borders have begun to resemble *vassals* who obey its every command.

The usually independent central bank became the *vassal* of special interest groups intent on keeping inflation low.

VAUNT *v.* (VAWNT) to brag about; to brag

The scientists wrote a paper *vaunting* their success in finding a vaccine for the measles.

After winning the game, the sports hero swaggered and *vaunted* in front of the cheerleaders.

VERBIAGE *n.* (VUHR bee ij) wordiness, too many words for the purpose; how words are used to express something, diction, wording

Nestled within the author's *verbiage* were a few well-chosen words describing her thesis.

Without scientific *verbiage*, a paper on medicine would be incomprehensible for any scholar.

VERDIGRIS *n.* (VUHR duh grees) green patina that forms on the outside of copper, brass or bronze exposed to air or the ocean

It was hard to imagine that the surface of the ancient sculpture, encrusted with *verdigris*, used to be shiny bronze.

VERNAL *adj.* (VUHR nuhl) occurring in spring; springlike; fresh, youthful

The *vernal* equinox occurs when the number of hours of darkness equals the number of hours of light, and is usually considered the first day of spring.

There is a pleasant quality to *vernal* sunshine which sets it apart from the burning summer sun.

The narcissus is one of the most prolific of the vernal flowers.

VIAND *n.* (VYE uhnd) an article or a kind of food; *pl.* viands

Most death row inmates choose to have T-bone steak as their last meal. It must be a bittersweet experience to be served this *viand* before going to die.

The table was loaded with *viands* of every kind, but the hostess could see that they would soon spoil if more people didn't arrive at the party.

QUICK QUIZ #63

Match each word in the first column with its definition in the second column. Check your answers in the back of the book.

1. undulate	a. slave
2. uxorious	b. green copper covering
3. vainglorious	c. brag
4. valetudinarian	d. doting on one's wife
5. vassal	e. wordiness
6. vaunt	f. food
7. verbiage	g. boastful
8. verdigris	h. springlike
9. vernal	i. infirm
10. viand	j. to move like a wave

VIRAGO *n.* (vi RAH goh) a shrew; a manly woman, a warrior

This word comes from the Latin "vir" (man) and was first used in English in an early translation of the Bible as the name given to Eve by Adam. Adam said that the being created out of his flesh would "be called *virago*, for she is taken of man." The word is used today to describe an impudent scold, a termagant.

The thugs had the bad luck to pick a fight with the young *virago* who easily dispatched the whole gang.

VIRIDESCENT *adj.* (vir uh DES uhnt) green

The reflection of the snow-covered peaks contrasted with the *viridescent* water of the pond.

VITREOUS *adj.* (VIH tree uhs) glasslike; made from glass

The spelunkers entered an enormous cavern resplendent with *vitreous* quartz that sparkled in the light of their flashlights.

The pot was covered with a *vitreous* glaze that would last virtually forever.

VITUPERATE *v.* (vye TOO puh rayt) or (vih TOO puh rayt) to revile, to scold harshly, to vilify

The virago, using language that could not be repeated here, *vituperated* the cab driver for running the red light.

The book *vituperated* the head of a Texas Savings and Loan as a thief, thus ending his career as a bank administrator.

VOIR DIRE *n.* (vwahr dihr) a preliminary questioning process to determine the suitability of prospective witnesses or jurors (also voire dire)

This word comes from the Latin "voir" (truth) and "dire" (to speak).

Fungerson, acting as his own lawyer, decided to skip the *voir dire* examination of the witness and get right to the questioning.

For celebrity trials the *voir dire* can take weeks.

VOTARY *n.* (VOHT uh ree) a committed worshiper; a zealously devoted person; an enthusiast

When it was revealed that Charlie Parker was alive and on tour in southwestern Alabama, *votaries* of jazz thronged to the concert.

WAGGISH *adj.* (WAG gish) jocular, wanton; a lover of jokes

Some *waggish* boys had vandalized the portrait of the president of the university in a thoroughly ingenious manner. Over a period of years, they had added paint, one dab at a time, until the sitter looked like Bela Lagosi.

The celebrations were of a *waggish* nature, with participants romping about yelling with good humored joy.

WEAL *n.* (WEEL) prosperity, well-being; the general good

Jackie Onasis knew that she had the love of the American people in *weal* and woe.

The increases in taxes will be good for the public *weal*, but bad for anyone who happens to be in the middle class.

WELTANSCHAUUNG *n.* (VELT AHN shaaw uhng) a complete philosophy of the universe, world view

The industrial revolution replaced a Christian *weltanschauung* with a scientific one.

Darwin's theories, while not immediately accepted, were instrumental in introducing the average biologist to an evolutionary *weltanschauung*.

WELTER *n.* (WEL tuhr) confusion v. (of a ship) to wallow as if on high seas; to roll like the sea; to sit soaking in a liquid

Her home had become a *welter* of newspapers and junk mail, as her furniture lay buried under two feet of recyclables.

The path he had remembered as a superhighway in his youth, was now a *welter* of brambles, impossible to pass.

The shipwrecked victims *weltered* in the ocean for three weeks in a tiny skiff with only five gallons of water.

The new owner of the company found himself *weltered* in the debt of his predecessor.

QUICK QUIZ #64

Match each word in the first column with its definition in the second column. Check your answers in the back of the book.

1. virago	a. confusion
2. viridescent	b. world view
3. vitreous	c. glasslike
4. vituperate	d. jocular
5. voir dire	e. shrew
6. votary	f. enthusiast
7. waggish	g. green
8. weal	h. questioning juries
9. Weltanschauung	i. to villify
10. welter	j. well-being

WELTSCHMERZ n. (VELT shmerts) world weariness

He was suffering from a *weltschmerz* brought on by two years of unemployment.

She was only sixteen, yet finding little interest in anything, she acted as if she was in a state of *weltschmerz*.

WONT adj. (WAWNT) accustomed, inclined n. habit, custom

All the excitement caused her to sleep longer than she was *wont*, and when she awoke, it was nearly lunch time.

He ate three apples and jumped up and down as he was *wont* to do before a performance.

WREAK v. (REEK) to inflict; to vent, to indulge; to cause

The storm *wreaked* vengeance on the godless sailors and their passenger Jonah until he consented to be thrown overboard.

After restraining his feelings for ten minutes, the boss finally *wreaked* his anger at a lowly secretary who happened to be in the wrong place at the wrong time.

A disastrous blizzard *wreaked* havoc on the small town.

WUNDERKIND n. (VAWN duh kint) a child with exceptional talent who becomes famous at an early age, a prodigy

The old guard of investment bankers had to make way for a generation of *wunderkinder*; adept with computers, these whiz-kids found ways to make money that mystified their elders.

Mozart, a *wunderkind* of immense talent, matured as a musician before he reached puberty.

ZAFTIG adj. (ZAHF tikh) having a shapely figure, full-bosomed (also zoftig)

This Yiddish word is derived from the German word for juicy.

All the *zaftig* sunbathers made a day at the beach a tortuous proposition for Carl.

ZEPHYR n. (ZEF uhr) a gentle breeze

On a beautiful spring day, a *zephyr* moved the leaves of the laurel tree in a lazy fashion.

ZIGGURAT n. (ZIG uh rat) a pyramid constructed by the ancient Assyrians and Babylonians

A ziggurat can be distinguished from an Egyptian pyramid because it was constructed of stages, each of which was smaller than the one below, so as to create balconies that seemed to step up the ziggurat.

The Tower of Babel was probably the most famous *ziggurat*.

QUICK QUIZ #65

Match each word in the first column with its definition in the second column.
Check your answers in the back of the book.

1. weltschmerz
2. wont
3. wreak
4. wunderkind
5. zaftig
6. zephyr
7. ziggurat

a. stepped pyramid
b. vent
c. world weariness
d. child prodigy
e. shapely
f. warm breeze
g. habit

Chapter 3

CRACKING CROSSWORD PUZZLES

HOW TO CRACK CROSSWORD PUZZLES

If you are like most people, you believe that the puzzles are a way of measuring your vocabulary or even your IQ. Maybe your aunt can do the Sunday *New York Times* puzzle in only an hour *in pen*, and you might wonder how she got to be so smart. The truth is, however, that just like anything else, being good at crossword puzzles is not about being smart. It's more about learning a few tricks and a select group of about fifty crossword puzzle words. If you read the next few pages and learn the accompanying words, you will find these puzzles much less daunting.

WE'RE TALKING AMERICAN CROSSWORD PUZZLES

There are a number of different types of puzzles, but we are going to discuss the American crossword puzzles that you will probably find in your local newspaper. In these, a definition or clue is provided, and you are responsible for coming up with a word to fill in the squares. The clues are not especially cryptic, but they are usually not simple definitions either.

THERE MUST BE A TRICK TO THESE

Beginning cruciverbalists are often mystified by these puzzles, but as you begin to do a few, they get easier. They provide a good exercise in word play and are sure to enhance your Scrabble game. To learn to think like the puzzle makers, there are certain little tricks you should know.

FILL IN THE BLANKS

These clues are often the easiest. Scan through the clues and do them first.

THE *S* TRICK

Some of the clues in the puzzle indicate that the answer is a plural. You can sometimes use this information to get a crossing word. Most, but not all, plurals end in the letter S. If the clue suggests a Greek or Latin word, however, it may not end in S.

THE WEIRD LETTER/CONSONANT TRICK

Once you get a word, look at any crossing words that fall on a consonant, especially if it is an uncommon letter like X or Q. Having a letter to start makes it much easier to reach an answer.

DON'T TAKE CLUES AT FACE VALUE

If the clue seems like a noun but still mystifies you, think verb. If it ends in a question mark, look for a pun. If it seems too easy, it probably is.

THEMES

Most puzzles today are arranged with a certain theme in mind. The long words in the puzzle are often related in some way. For example, they might all contain the name of a color or a particular word or they might form a phrase. If you can figure out the theme and find the long words, the rest of the puzzle will be much easier.

WHERE DO THEY GET THOSE WORDS?

Although it might seem that a crossword puzzle creator could use any word in the English language, the structure of the puzzle severely limits the types of words that they can actually use. You will find that as you do more and more puzzles, certain words will appear over and over again. To be good at crossword puzzles, you must know these words. Some of these are fairly common—"one" is a favorite of puzzle constructors—but many are rare and only used in crosswords. If you can learn the fifty most common of these puzzle words, you will find the rest of the puzzle much more manageable.

HONEY, PASS THE OLEO

Perhaps the most common crossword puzzle word is "oleo," which is either a bread spread or a butter substitute. "Why 'oleo'?" you might ask. The answer is that "oleo" has several vowels of which the crossword puzzle creators are so fond. The problem is that few people use "oleo" in normal conversation (unless you're from Michigan or Wisconsin).

A LEG UP

The following list is of the most common crossword puzzle words. We have weeded through hundreds of puzzles to find the words that come up again and again, and that are so rare that you might not know them. If you take some time to learn these words, the puzzles will seem a lot more fun.

IT'S NOT CHEATING . . . REALLY

Many feel that using any aid, especially a crossword puzzle dictionary, while solving the puzzle is like peeking at the answers in the back of a book. But by learning these words, you are simply putting yourself on an equal footing with the creators. There is no reason (outside of puzzledom) that you should be expected to know that an "etui" is a case for small grooming articles. If you learn these words, you will be able to concentrate more fully on the fun parts of the puzzle.

THE LIST

ade	(AYD) a drink made with citrus juice, water, and sugar
adit	(A diht) mine entrance
AFL	first half of AFL-CIO, labor union
agora	(AH guh ruh) a market in ancient Greece
Agra	(AH gruh) an Indian City where the Taj Mahal is located; a carpet made in Agra
amah	(AH muh) an Eastern wet-nurse
ameer	(ih MIR) a variation of emir, Middle Eastern ruler
Amin	(AH meen) Idi Amin, former dictator of Uganda
amir	(ih MIR) one of several variations of emir
aria	(AHR ee uh) a melody sung by a soloist in an opera (The clue for this word is often some diva or other's piece or song)
CIO	second half of AFL-CIO, labor Union
Clio	(KLEE oh) the muse of History
Cree	(KREE) a Native American people located in the Midwest from Ontario to Montana
Deere	(DEER) tractor manufacturer
Dele	(DEE lee) to delete (a character or word) from a manuscript
Edo	(EE doh) former name for Tokyo, Japan
Eire	(AR uh) or (ER) archaic name for Ireland
Eli	(EE lie) student from Yale
em	(EM) printer's measure
emeer	(ih MIR) another variation of emir
emir	(ih MIR) Middle Eastern ruler

en	(EN) printer's measure
enero	(eh NEH roh) January in Spanish
épée	(EH pay) fencing sword
ern(e)	(UHRN) sea eagle
ess	(ES) something, like a curve, that resembles an S.
été	(AY tay) summer in French
etui	(ay TWEE) a case for small articles (nail clippers, needles, etc.) that are used often
Iago	(ee AH go) villian in Othello
Idi	(EE dee) Idi Amin, former dictator of Uganda
lese majesty	(LEEZ maj ihs tee) a crime commited against the sovereign of a state; an insult to another person's dignity (usually clued as "—— majesty")
oleo	(OH lee oh) margarine
olla	(AH luh) olla porida is a type of stew; an earthenware jar
omer	(OH muhr) Hebrew counting measure
ort	(AWRT) scrap, refuse
Oto	(OHD oh) a Native American people from Nebraska
proa	(PROH uh) Indonesian boat; light sailing craft (also prahu, prau, prow, praw)
snee	(SNEE) used in the phrase "snick or snee" which means to cut and parry with a knife
steno	(STE noh) one who takes dictation
stet	(STET) to mark that an alledged error marked to be corrected should be left as is
stile	(STYEL) steps over a fence
stoa	(STOH uh) Greek portico
Syne	(SYEN) end of the title of the song "Auld Lang Syne"
Thalia	(THAYL ya) the Greek muse of comedy
Ural	(YOO ruhl) mountains in Eastern Europe
veep	(VEEP) nickname for vice president

FORMIC PHRASES AND SUCH

Although you might think that it is enough to know that a bear is a bear, there are specific words in the English languange to describe someone or something that is bear-like (ursine) and to describe a group of bears (a sloth of bears). These terms of venery (of the hunt) are fanciful and precise and allow the modern wordmonger to use the right term for any beastly occasion.

Animal	Term of Venery	Having the animals characteristics
ants	a colony of ants	formic
apes	a shrewdness of apes	
asses	a pass of asses	asinine
bears	a sloth of bears	ursine
bees	a swarm of bees	
caterpillars	an army of caterpillars	
cats	a clowder of cats	
	a cluster of housecats	
	a clutter of cats	
	a destruction of wildcats	
	a kindle of kittens	
cattle	a drove of cattle	bovine
chickens	a brood of hens	
	a run of poultry	
crows	a murder of crows	corvine
dogs	a cowardice of curs	
	a kennel of dogs	
	a leash of greyhounds	
	a litter of pups	
	a mute of hounds	
	a pack of dogs	
ducks	a paddling of ducks	
	a team of ducks (in flight)	
eagles	a convocation of eagles	aquiline
eggs	a clutch of eggs	
elephants	a herd of elephants	
elk	a gang of elk	

ferrets	a business of ferrets	
finches	a charm of finches	
fish	a catch of fish (when dead)	piscine
	a school of fish (when swimming)	
flies	a business of flies	
foxes	a skulk of foxes	vulpine/ vixen
	(for female)	
geese	a gaggle of geese	anserine
	a skein of geese (in flight)	
goats	a trip of goats	hircine
grasshoppers	a cloud of grasshoppers	
hawks	a cast of hawks	accipitrine
hogs	a drift of hogs	porcine
horses	a field of racehorses	equine
	a herd of horses	
	a string of ponies	
jellyfish	a smack of jellyfish	
kangaroo	a mob of kangaroo	
lapwings	a deceit of lapwings	
larks	an exaltation of larks	
leopards	a leap of leopards	
lions	a pride of lions	leonine
locusts	a plague of locusts	
moles	a labor of moles	
monkeys	a barrel of monkeys	simian
mules	a barren of mules	
owls	a parliament of owls	
oxen	a team of oxen	
parrots	a company of parrots	
partridge	a covey of partridge	
peacocks	an ostentation of peacocks	pavonine
pheasants	a nye of pheasants	
rabbits	a colony of rabbits	
	a husk of hare	

ravens	an unkindness of ravens	
rhinoceroses	a crash of rhinoceroses	
seals	a pod of seals	
sheep	a flock of sheep	ovine
snakes	a nest of vipers	ophidian
sparrows	a host of sparrows	
squirrels	a dray of squirrels	
swallows	a flight of swallows	hirundine
toads	a knot of toads	
turtledoves	a true love of turtledoves	
wasps	a nest of wasps	
whales	a gam of whales	
wolves	a route of wolves	lupine

Chapter 4

THE FINAL EXAMS

FINAL EXAM DRILL 1

Definitions

For each question below, match the word on the left with its definition on the right.

1. syllogism		a. combined Forces stronger than individual
2. eugenics		b. human breeding
3. muckrake		c. purchased complement
4. parlance		d. biological partition
5. synergy		e. confirm
6. trade-last		f. deductive reasoning
7. protean		g. expose misconduct
8. septum		h. diction
9. handsel		i. good luck gift
10. homologate		j. taking on many shapes

FINAL EXAM DRILL 2

Associations

For each question below, match the word on the left with the word most similar in meaning on the right.

1. spelunker		a. claque
2. termagant		b. incunabula
3. toady		c. verbiage
4. prolix		d. troglodyte
5. poltroon		e. votary
6. effluvium		f. halitosis
7. defalcate		g. gallivant
8. élan		h. peculate
9. Panglossian		i. welter
10. coquet		j. Pollyanna
11. hugger-mugger		k. virago
12. antediluvian		l. recreant

FINAL EXAM DRILL 3

Definitions

For each question below, match the word on the left with its definition on the right.

1. epigone
2. pharisaical
3. integument
4. abreaction
5. crapulous
6. pulchritude
7. opus
8. ensconce
9. deconstruction
10. vassal

a. envelope
b. system of philosophy that assumes nothing
c. catharsis
d. overindulgence
e. hypercritical
f. imitator
g. creative work
h. to sunggle
i. slave
j. beauty

FINAL EXAM DRILL 4

Definitions

For each question below, match the word on the left with its definition on the right.

1. fillip
2. Ockham's razor
3. theosophy
4. striated
5. sinecure
6. scalawag
7. ethnocentric
8. précis
9. quiddity
10. provenance
11. onus
12. Procrustean
13. salacious

a. origin
b. essense
c. requiring strict conFormity
d. easy job
e. burden
f. scamp
g. snap
h. easiest is best
i. ethnic supremacy
j. lustful
k. abstract
l. lined
m. belief in meditation

FINAL EXAM DRILL 5

Definitions

For each question below, match the word on the left with its definition on the right.

1. captious	a. rough
2. Nimrod	b. redistrict unfairly
3. phlegmatic	c. hypercritical
4. manumit	d. semantics
5. scabrous	e. hunter
6. caduceus	f. Hermes staff
7. mien	g. free from bondage
8. semiotics	h. bearing
9. gerrymander	i. calm
10. docent	j. tour guide

FINAL EXAM DRILL 6

Associations

For each question below, match the word on the left with the word most similar in meaning on the right.

1. Philippic	a. saturnine
2. pinguid	b. Sybaritic
3. badinage	c. thrall
4. éclat	d. dither
5. chattel	e. confabulate
6. metonymy	f. trope
7. bavardage	g. persiflage
8. eudaemonism	h. smarmy
9. commove	i. fulgent
10. dyspeptic	j. screed

FINAL EXAM DRILL 7

Definitions

For each question below, match the word on the left with its definition on the right.

1. epistolary		a.	cutter of gems
2. pertinacious		b.	showy
3. prandial		c.	rainy
4. merkin		d.	about letters
5. fulsome		e.	wig For pubic hair
6. pluvious		f.	obstinate
7. froufrou		g.	related to a meal
8. interdict		h.	offensively excessive
9. lapidary		i.	counterbalanced
10. equipoise		j.	prohibit

FINAL EXAM DRILL 8

Associations

For each question below, match the word on the left with the word most nearly its opposite on the right.

1. kudos		a.	rakehell
2. lassitude		b.	probity
3. mensch		c.	schlemiel
4. mettle		d.	sub-rosa
5. macerate		e.	tony
6. politic		f.	truculent
7. fabulist		g.	ossify
8. stentorian		h.	strappado
9. tatterdemalion		i.	tawdry
10. hoi polloi		j.	snollygoster

FINAL EXAM DRILL 9

Definitions

For each question below, match the word on the left with its definition on the right.

1. demimonde	a. burning at the stake
2. arrogate	b. curse
3. umbrage	c. a ritualistic drink
4. libation	d. a continual lawbreaker
5. dirigible	e. blimp
6. imprecate	f. displeasure
7. auto-da-fé	g. netherworld
8. lachrymose	h. weaping
9. fugacious	i. to appropriate
10. scofflaw	j. passing

FINAL EXAM DRILL 10

Definitions

For each question below, match the word on the left with its definition on the right.

1. qua	a. a teacher
2. solipsism	b. damnation
3. palindrome	c. focus on self
4. pedagogue	d. confuse
5. sibilant	e. daily
6. discombobulate	f. the "s" sound
7. perdition	g. word is same backwards
8. boilerplate	h. in the capacity of
9. gonif	i. Formulaic language
10. circadian	j. thief

FINAL EXAM DRILL 11

Associations

For each question below, match the word on the left with the word most similar in meaning on the right.

1. jejune	a. succubus
2. dybbuk	b. specie
3. stygian	c. mingy
4. cockalorum	d. vaunt
5. scintilla	e. tenebrous
6. clamant	f. sere
7. numismatics	g. plangent
8. exiguous	h. nadir
9. pillory	i. soupçon
10. mudsill	j. twit

FINAL EXAM DRILL 12

Definitions

For each question below, match the word on the left with its definition on the right.

1. sashay	a. group chained in line
2. concubinage	b. belief in all gods
3. Pablum	c. jam session
4. hootenanny	d. minimize
5. coffle	e. baby gruel
6. cincture	f. cohabitation
7. gloze	g. to glide
8. marplot	h. one who wrecks plans
9. pantheism	i. enclosure
10. puce	j. gray purple

FINAL EXAM DRILL 13

Pronunciations

Pronounce each of the following words without looking at column a or column b. Then select the column that comes closer to your pronunciation.

		Column A	Column B
1.	patois	PAY tohs	PA twah
2.	couvade	koo VAYD	koo VAHD
3.	sough	SOH	SAOW
4.	pusillanimous	pyoo suh LAN uh muhs	poo see LAN uh muhs
5.	lebensraum	LEB uhns ra oom	LAY benz ra oom
6.	ecce homo	e chay HOH moh	eh kay HOH moh
7.	ethos	EE thaws	EH thohs
8.	rapprochement	ra PROHS muhnt	ra prohsh MAH
9.	pasquinade	PAHS kwuh nahd	pas kwuh NAYD
10.	bathos	BAY thahs	BAH thohs

FINAL EXAM DRILL 14

Definitions

For each question below, match the word on the left with its definition on the right.

1. ruck	a. traitor
2. slatternly	b. tendency
3. abecedarian	c. all the gods
4. prestidigitation	d. suitcase
5. dingle	e. sleight of hand
6. pantheon	f. squalid
7. inchoate	g. alphabetical
8. quisling	h. incipient
9. proclivity	i. wooded valley
10. portmanteau	j. mass

FINAL EXAM DRILL 15

Definitions

For each question below, match the word on the left with its definition on the right.

1. bailiwick		a.	iconoclastic
2. pilcrow		b.	a hint
3. panjandrum		c.	expertise
4. tincture		d.	science of interpretation
5. hermeneutics		e.	nonsense
6. mordant		f.	rear
7. dorsal		g.	blood pressure measurer
8. sphygmomanometer		h.	self-important person
9. heterodox		i.	¶
10. dada		j.	incisive

FINAL EXAM DRILL 16

Definitions

For each question below, match the word on the left with its definition on the right.

1. voir dire		a.	eager
2. canoodle		b.	questioning juries
3. agog		c.	caress
4. pathetic fallacy		d.	chew
5. masticate		e.	juvenile
6. prophylaxis		f.	perForming miracles
7. puerile		g.	prevention of disease
8. thaumaturgy		h.	slavish
9. sequacious		i.	anthropomorphism
10. chiaroscuro		j.	painting style with light and dark

FINAL EXAM DRILL 17

Definitions

For each question below, match the word on the left with its definition on the right.

1. avatar	a. malleable
2. atrabilious	b. establish
3. rime	c. archetype
4. crotchet	d. study of knowledge
5. predicate	e. domain
6. gymnosophist	f. coating of ice
7. ductile	g. peevish
8. factitious	h. nude meditators
9. epistemology	i. man made
10. demesne	j. whimsical notion

FINAL EXAM DRILL 18

Definitions

For each question below, match the word on the left with its definition on the right.

1. musth	a. threatening
2. barrator	b. censor
3. bowdlerize	c. mix up
4. contraindicate	d. elephant frenzy
5. minatory	e. tomboy
6. mulct	f. defiant
7. embrangle	g. coup
8. hoyden	h. fine
9. obstreperous	i. ambulance chaser
10. putsch	j. hurt

FINAL EXAM DRILL 19

Pronunciations

Pronounce each of the following words without looking at column a or column b. Then select the column that comes closer to your pronunciation.

		Column A	Column B
1.	etiology	eh tee AHL uh jee	eed ee AHL uh jee
2.	dudgeon	DUH juhn	DUHD juhn
3.	paean	PAY uhn	PEE uhn
4.	borborygmus	BOHR bohr muhs	bawr buh RIG muhs
5.	sui generis	swee JUH nuhr ee	soo eye JEH nuhr is
6.	beguine	BEE gwyen	be GEEN or bay GEEN
7.	lucre	LOO kruh	LOO kuhr
8.	obloquy	ahb LOH kee	AHB luh kwee
9.	leitmotif	LET moh teef	lyet moh TEEF
10.	Weltanschauung	WELT uhn shahw uhng	VELT AHN shaaw uhng

FINAL EXAM DRILL 20

Definitions

For each question below, match the word on the left with its definition on the right.

1. redoubtable	a. Formidable
2. wont	b. suffocate
3. schlimazel	c. a vacillator
4. meniscus	d. habit
5. mugwump	e. crescent shaped body
6. googol	f. huge number
7. kibitz	g. partisan
8. burke	h. empiricism
9. tendentious	i. give advice unasked
10. positivism	j. unlucky simp

FINAL EXAM DRILL 21

Associations

For each question below, match the word on the left with the word most similar in meaning on the right.

1. donnish
2. niggle
3. birkie
4. coxcomb
5. groak
6. absinthe
7. agathism
8. ersatz
9. sapid
10. balderdash

a. grig
b. repast
c. prig
d. pettifogger
e. meliorism
f. bilge
g. viridescent
h. fop
i. mimetic
j. toothsome

FINAL EXAM DRILL 22

Definitions

For each question below, match the word on the left with its definition on the right.

1. primogeniture
2. deliquesce
3. sobriquet
4. libidinous
5. eurythmics
6. bower
7. somnambulist
8. filibuster
9. effete
10. weal

a. lascivious
b. first born
c. depleted
d. obstructive speech
e. cottage
f. melt away
g. well-being
h. sleepwalker
i. dancing
j. nickname

FINAL EXAM DRILL 23

Definitions

For each question below, match the word on the left with its definition on the right.

1.	nonplus	a.	heart shaped
2.	nacre	b.	bewilder
3.	Pyrrhic	c.	connoisseur
4.	iterant	d.	mother-of-pearl
5.	codicil	e.	springlike
6.	cognoscente	f.	a costly victory
7.	vernal	g.	repeating
8.	cordiForm	h.	something nourishing
9.	restive	i.	appendix of will
10.	pabulum	j.	stubborn

FINAL EXAM DRILL 24

Pronunciations

Pronounce each of the following words without looking at column a or column b. Then select the column that comes closer to your pronunciation.

		Column A	Column B
1.	fustian	FUHS tee uhn	FUHS chuhn
2.	palaver	PAH lah vuhr	puh LAV uhr
3.	desuetude	duh SWEY tood	DES wee tood
4.	demarche	duh MARK	day MAHRSH
5.	outré	oo TRAY	OWT ruh
6.	detritus	DEH tri tuhs	duh TRYED uhs
7.	deism	DYE izm	DEE iz uhm
8.	oeuvre	EUVR	OOV ruh
9.	sangfroid	sang FRWAH	SANG froid
10.	behemoth	buh HEE muth	BEE hee moth

FINAL EXAM DRILL 25

Definitions

For each question below, match the word on the left with its definition on the right.

1.	dormition	a.	picture puzzle
2.	bodkin	b.	sleep of death
3.	numinous	c.	antithesis
4.	desiderate	d.	spiritual
5.	rebus	e.	whereness
6.	motile	f.	desire
7.	ubiety	g.	able to move
8.	chthonic	h.	related to netherworld
9.	contradistinction	i.	curtsy
10.	genuflect	j.	hole maker

FINAL EXAM DRILL 26

Definitions

For each question below, match the word on the left with its definition on the right.

1.	titivate	a.	medley
2.	raffish	b.	decorate
3.	teleology	c.	opera singer
4.	zephyr	d.	long word
5.	sesquipedalian	e.	study of purpose
6.	diva	f.	tawdry
7.	kvetch	g.	dwarf
8.	salmagundi	h.	to complain
9.	fusty	i.	musty
10.	homunculus	j.	warm breeze

FINAL EXAM DRILL 27

Definitions

For each question below, match the word on the left with its definition on the right.

1. concupiscence		a.	humming sound
2. sine qua non		b.	correct
3. saccadic		c.	something essential
4. emend		d.	magical
5. delphian		e.	obscurely prophetic
6. bombilation		f.	lust
7. palimpsest		g.	whip
8. sessile		h.	sedentary
9. fey		i.	erased parchment
10. flagellate		j.	jerky

FINAL EXAM DRILL 28

Distinctions

For each question below, match the word on the left with the word most nearly its opposite on the right.

1. ablution		a.	rectitude
2. affective		b.	cognitive
3. akimbo		c.	paramour
4. apogee		d.	nebbish
5. acidulous		e.	martinet
6. beldam		f.	minx
7. bête noire		g.	tintinnabulation
8. bonhomie		h.	propinquity
9. bumptious		i.	beamish
10. chirr		j.	sully

FINAL EXAM DRILL 29

Definitions

For each question below, match the word on the left with its definition on the right.

1. hirsute
2. quaff
3. recherché
4. perorate
5. neoteric
6. fleer
7. craquelure
8. caducity
9. puissance
10. modicum

a. modern
b. make a long speech
c. cracks on oil paintings
d. power
e. rare
f. a wee bit
g. hairy
h. senility
i. sneer
j. drink

FINAL EXAM DRILL 30

Definitions

For each question below, match the word on the left with its definition on the right.

1. garrote
2. peen
3. legerdemain
4. bibulous
5. tor
6. conation
7. dalliance
8. spoonerism
9. dyad
10. ziggurat

a. manual dexterity
b. will
c. transposing of letters in words
d. strangle
e. flirtation
f. drunken
g. pair
h. ball shaped end of hammer
i. rocky crag
j. stepped pyramid

FINAL EXAM DRILL 31

Definitions

For each question below, match the word on the left with its definition on the right.

1.	consanguinity	a.	missing part
2.	bunkum	b.	clear
3.	omphaloskepsis	c.	inferior
4.	pellucid	d.	false boasting
5.	zaftig	e.	focal point
6.	déclassé	f.	shapely
7.	jactitation	g.	related
8.	gestalt	h.	claptrap
9.	cynosure	i.	wholeness
10.	lacuna	j.	navel meditating

FINAL EXAM DRILL 32

Pronunciations

Pronounce each of the following words without looking at column a or column b. Then select the column that comes closer to your pronunciation.

		Column A	Column B
1.	pace	PAYS	PAY see
2.	susurrate	suh SUH rayt	SUH suh rayt
3.	sapient	SAY pee uhnt	SAH pee uhnt
4.	daedal	DAY ee duhl	DEE duhl
5.	phylogeny	fye LAH juh nee	fuh LAH juh nee
6.	renascent	REH nuh sahnt	RIH na suhnt
7.	bedizen	beh DYE zuhn	BEH duh zuhn
8.	aleatory	AH lee a toh ree	AY lee a toh ree
9.	hagiography	HA jee uh gra fee	HA gee uh gra fee
10.	glabrous	GLAH bruhs	GLAY bruhs

FINAL EXAM DRILL 33

Definitions

For each question below, match the word on the left with its definition on the right.

1. devolution
2. luftmensch
3. penumbra
4. dewy-eyed
5. roister
6. edacious
7. ululate
8. gird
9. decollate
10. determinism

a. voracious
b. shadow
c. everything is caused
d. howl
e. decentralization
f. encircle
g. behead
h. swagger
i. naive
j. dreamer

FINAL EXAM DRILL 34

Definitions

For each question below, match the word on the left with its definition on the right.

1. feral
2. nabob
3. juggernaut
4. lickspittle
5. retinue
6. parvenu
7. bibelot
8. nimbus
9. hypomania
10. truckle

a. attendants
b. abject bootlicker
c. trinket
d. be servile
e. cloud
f. governor
g. social climber
h. wild
i. crushing vehicle
j. feeling of elation

FINAL EXAM DRILL 35

Definitions

For each question below, match the word on the left with its definition on the right.

1. mollycoddle		a.	outside adviser in a court case
2. manqué		b.	noxious vapor
3. diaphanous		c.	unfulfilled in reaching goals
4. deteriorism		d.	mafia
5. canard		e.	translucent
6. crepitate		f.	pessimism
7. miasma		g.	crackle
8. amicus curiae		h.	declare
9. camorra		i.	to pamper
10. aver		j.	tall tale

FINAL EXAM DRILL 36

Pronunciations

Pronounce each of the following words without looking at column a or column b. Then select the column that comes closer to your pronunciation.

		Column A	Column B
1.	aegis	AY ee juhs	EE juhs
2.	roué	ROO	roo AY or ROO ay
3.	Sturm und Drang	stoorm uhn DRAHNG	shtoor moont DRAHNG
4.	supernal	soo PUHRN uhl	SOO puhr nuhl
5.	verdigris	VUHR duh greez	VUHR duh grees
6.	uxorious	YOOK soh ree uhs	uhk SOH ree uhs
7.	ontogeny	AHN tuh je nee	ahn TUH juh nee
8.	scion	SKYE uhn	SYE uhn
9.	abstemious	abz TEE mee us	abz TEM ee uhs
10.	cachinnate	KA chuh nayt	KA kuh nayt

FINAL EXAM DRILL 37

Definitions

For each question below, match the word on the left with its definition on the right.

1. undulate
2. caryatid
3. epiphany
4. tectonic
5. tome
6. hobson's choice
7. arriviste
8. plenipotentiary
9. defenestration
10. popinjay

a. sudden understanding
b. relating to Earth's crust
c. having complete powers
d. a limited choice
e. big book
f. column
g. vain talker
h. to move like a wave
i. vulgar social climber
j. throw out a window

FINAL EXAM DRILL 38

Definitions

For each question below, match the word on the left with its definition on the right.

1. habeas corpus
2. catachresis
3. nefandous
4. poultice
5. sabulous
6. prognosticate
7. onanism
8. waggish
9. recusant
10. Cassandra

a. predict
b. unheeded prophet
c. gunk used to heal
d. non-conformist
e. order giving prisoner second chance
f. sandy
g. misuse of word
h. abominable
i. jocular
j. masturbation

FINAL EXAM DRILL 39

Definitions

For each question below, match the word on the left with its definition on
the right.

1. heuristic
2. froward
3. apodictic
4. dissonance
5. solecism
6. myrmidon
7. serif
8. picayune
9. eschatology
10. threnody

a. contrary
b. discord
c. incontrovertible
d. violation of grammar
e. speculative
f. belief in the last judgement
g. tiny
h. dirge
i. fine lines on letters
j. faithful follower

FINAL EXAM DRILL 40

Definitions

For each question below, match the word on the left with its definition on
the right.

1. theodicy
2. cenobite
3. empiricism
4. mountebank
5. condign
6. nictate
7. codex
8. niggardly
9. dauphin
10. throttlebottom

a. wink
b. member of a convent
c. appropriate
d. eldest son of King of France
e. volume
f. nostrom hawker
g. stingy
h. experience is supreme
i. God really is good
j. bad vice-president

FINAL EXAM DRILL 41

Pronunciations
Pronounce each of the following words without looking at column a or column b. Then select the column that comes closer to your pronunciation.

	Column A	Column B
1. Charybdis	chah RIB duhs	kuh RIB duhs
2. priapic	prye A pik	pree A pik
3. réclame	ruh KLAYM	ray KLAM
4. educe	ee DYOOS	eh DYOOS
5. otiose	OH shee ohs	OH tee uhs
6. sui juris	SWEE joo ris	soo eye JOO ris
7. reify	RAY uh fye	REE uh fye
8. fusillade	FYOO suh lahd	FYOO suh layd
9. ombudsman	AHM boodz muhn	ahm BUHDZ muhn
10. nepenthe	nih PENTH	ni PEN thee

FINAL EXAM DRILL 42

Definitions
For each question below, match the word on the left with its definition on the right.

1. encaustic	a. abrupt halt in speech
2. dowager	b. irritable
3. aposiopesis	c. bougeoise
4. paronomasia	d. widow with husband's money
5. degauss	e. demagnetise
6. eponymous	f. hot wax painting
7. splenetic	g. named after
8. Babbitt	h. pun
9. posit	i. triffle
10. bagatelle	j. postulate

FINAL EXAM DRILL 43

Definitions

For each question below, match the word on the left with its definition on the right.

1. pastiche	a. to slave
2. cuckold	b. a break
3. encomium	c. fusion of philosophy
4. febrile	d. cheated on man
5. cachet	e. feverish
6. interregnum	f. mark of distinction
7. syncretism	g. primary principle
8. disabuse	h. undeceive
9. dharma	i. panegyric
10. moil	j. satirical piece

FINAL EXAM DRILL 44

Pronunciations

Pronounce each of the following words without looking at column a or column b. Then select the column that comes closer to your pronunciation.

		Column A	Column B
1.	synecdoche	sih NEK duh kee	SIH nek duh chee
2.	tarantism	TAR uhn tiz uhm	tar AN tiz uhm
3.	boîte	bwaht	BOOT
4.	satrap	SAY trap	SAH trap
5.	igneous	IG nee uhs	IG neh uhs
6.	Grand Guignol	grand gweeg NAHL	grahn geen YAWL
7.	hegira	heh JYE ruh	heh JEE ruh
8.	wunderkind	VAWN duh kint	WUN duhr kihnd
9.	divagate	DEE vuh gayt	DIH vuh gayt
10.	nostrum	NOH struhm	NAHS truhm

FINAL EXAM DRILL 45

Definitions

For each question below, match the word on the left with its definition on the right.

1. pudency	a. bog
2. exculpate	b. modesty
3. hortative	c. academic
4. quagmire	d. wood like
5. valetudinarian	e. acquit
6. bissextile day	f. dungeon
7. sylvan	g. infirm
8. moot	h. one sense inForms the other
9. synesthesia	i. Feb. 29
10. oubliette	j. encouraging

FINAL EXAM DRILL 46

Definitions

For each question below, match the word on the left with its definition on the right.

1. bray	a. universal
2. lubricious	b. cudgeling
3. pleonasm	c. needing continual efFort
4. eschew	d. soil
5. ecumenical	e. replaceable
6. fungible	f. waste time
7. bastinado	g. redundancy
8. fribble	h. shun
9. Sisyphean	i. crush
10. besmirch	j. slippery

FINAL EXAM DRILL 47

Definitions

For each question below, match the word on the left with its definition on the right.

1. gad
2. structuralism
3. esurient
4. ontology
5. argot
6. gobbet
7. hullabaloo
8. elision
9. hustings
10. rubric

a. place For speeches
b. greedy
c. class or category
d. uproar
e. dialect
f. wander
g. omitting a sound
h. breaking down of phenomenon
i. chunk
j. study of being

FINAL EXAM DRILL 48

Definitions

For each question below, match the word on the left with its definition on the right.

1. dolor
2. immure
3. lithe
4. extirpate
5. epicene
6. adumbrate
7. tergiversate
8. fetid
9. simulacrum
10. amaranth

a. sorrow
b. flower that lasts Forever
c. graceful
d. Foreshadow
e. stinky
f. destroy
g. entomb
h. image
i. hermaphroditic
j. equivocate

FINAL EXAM DRILL 49

Pronunciations

Pronounce each of the following words without looking at column a or column b. Then select the column that comes closer to your pronunciation.

		Column A	Column B
1.	imbroglio	uhm BROHL yoh	im BROHG lee oh
2.	schadenfreude	SHAH duhn froy duh	SHAH duhn froid
3.	viand	VEE uhnd	VYE uhnd
4.	adjure	ad JUR	uh JUR
5.	wreak	REEK	REHK
6.	riposte	RIH pohst	ri POHST
7.	farrago	FA rah goh	fuh RAH goh
8.	weltschmerz	VELT shmerts	WELT shmertz
9.	imago	uh MAY goh	IH mah goh
10.	psephology	see FAHL uh jee	seh FAHL uh jee

FINAL EXAM DRILL 50

Definitions

For each question below, match the word on the left with its definition on the right.

1.	assignation	a.	tolerate
2.	moue	b.	crown
3.	brook	c.	tryst
4.	plenary	d.	metropolitan area
5.	aphasia	e.	verve
6.	panache	f.	inability to express ideas
7.	conurbation	g.	full
8.	lariat	h.	lasso
9.	ailurophile	i.	cat lover
10.	diadem	j.	pout

FINAL EXAM DRILL 51

Definitions

For each question below, match the word on the left with its definition on the right.

1. comity
2. absquatulate
3. opisthenar
4. fractious
5. dégagé
6. quidnunc
7. trice
8. gevalt
9. contumacious
10. charnel

a. Darn!
b. cranky
c. rebellious
d. courtesy
e. a short time
f. busybody
g. to decamp
h. back of the hand
i. casual
j. tomb

FINAL EXAM DRILL 52

Definitions

For each question below, match the word on the left with its definition on the right.

1. chary
2. cupidity
3. vainglorious
4. ablate
5. sedulous
6. Diaspora
7. vitreous
8. colophon
9. banausic
10. miscreant

a. cautious
b. publisher's trademark
c. painstaking
d. villian
e. mechanical
f. dispersion of Jews
g. covetousness
h. boastful
i. wear away
j. glasslike

FINAL EXAM DRILL 53

Distinctions

For each question below, match the word on the left with the word most nearly its opposite on the right.

1. atavism
2. coruscate
3. dasein
4. agnate
5. doggerel
6. eleemosynary
7. dulcet
8. etiolated
9. clerisy
10. flagitious

a. penurious
b. eruct
c. distaff
d. rubescent
e. turgid
f. gamin
g. gemütlich
h. crepuscular
i. coeval
j. nugatory

FINAL EXAM DRILL 54

Definitions

For each question below, match the word on the left with its definition on the right.

1. comport
2. cortege
3. décolletage
4. tumescence
5. feckless
6. celerity
7. ideate
8. rostrum
9. prognathous
10. objurgate

a. protruding
b. pulpit
c. retinue
d. imagine
e. ineffective
f. to scold
g. swelling
h. neckline
i. behave
j. swiftness

FINAL EXAM DRILL 55

Definitions
For each question below, match the word on the left with its definition on the right.

1. poniard   a. repeat
2. tyro   b. senior member
3. sartorial   c. later
4. bruit   d. related to clothing
5. diphthong   e. beginner
6. donnybrook   f. nice butt
7. doyenne   g. brawl
8. callipygian   h. dagger
9. phenomenology   i. aieee
10. anon   j. philosophy of intuition

FINAL EXAM DRILL 56

Definitions
For each question below, match the word on the left with its definition on the right.

1. svelte   a. group
2. nascent   b. something that arrouses sympathy
3. gemeinschaft   c. to wear away
4. labile   d. doctrine of free will
5. in situ   e. adapatable
6. diacritical   f. distinguishing
7. cunctation   g. thin
8. excoriate   h. emerging
9. pathos   i. in place
10. indeterminism   j. procrastination

FINAL EXAM DRILL 57

Definitions

For each question below, match the word on the left with its definition on the right.

1. diddle
2. vituperate
3. penultimate
4. anomie
5. amanuensis
6. purview
7. jape
8. immolate
9. sallow
10. Decalogue

a. joke
b. next to last
c. stenographer
d. greenish
e. sacrifice
f. ten commandments
g. social instability
h. range
i. to cheat
j. to villify

THE ANSWERS

PRELIMINARY EXAM 1

1. b
2. a
3. b
4. b
5. a
6. a
7. b
8. a
9. b
10 b
11. b
12. a
13. a
14. b
15. b
16. b
17. a
18. b
19. b
20. b

PRELIMINARY EXAM 2

1. f
2. d
3. g
4. a
5. i
6. h
7. e
9. b
10. c

PRELIMINARY EXAM 3

1. c
2. a
3. h
4. g
5. i
6. e
7. d
9. f
10. b

Preliminary Exam 4

1. c
2. d
3. b
4. f
5. g
6. e
7. h
9. a
10. i

Preliminary Exam 5

1. h
2. e
3. a
4. f
5. b
6. i
7. c
9. d
10. g

Quick Quiz 1

1. j
2. a
3. g
4. i
5. h
6. e
7. d
8. f
9. b
10. c

Quick Quiz 2

1. a
2. j
3. b
4. e
5. c
6. d
7. i
8. g
9. h
10. f

Quick Quiz 3

1. g
2. a
3. d
4. j
5. h
6. f
7. b
8. e
9. c
10. i

Quick Quiz 4

1. h
2. e
3. c
4. b
5. g
6. d
7. i
8. j
9. a
10. f

QUICK QUIZ 5

1. i
2. a
3. j
4. d
5. c
6. g
7. e
8. h
9. f
10. b

QUICK QUIZ 6

1. j
2. a
3. d
4. e
5. b
6. f
7. c
8. g
9. i
10. h

QUICK QUIZ 7

1. b
2. i
3. c
4. e
5. h
6. g
7. a
8. d
9. j
10. f

QUICK QUIZ 8

1. a
2. j
3. c
4. i
5. d
6. g
7. f
8. e
9. b
10. h

QUICK QUIZ 9

1. e
2. h
3. d
4. b
5. c
6. i
7. a
8. g
9. j
10. f

QUICK QUIZ 10

1. j
2. a
3. c
4. i
5. f
6. e
7. d
8. h
9. g
10. b

QUICK QUIZ 11

1. e
2. a
3. f
4. d
5. b
6. g
7. j
8. h
9. c
10. i

QUICK QUIZ 12

1. f
2. d
3. b
4. a
5. i
6. g
7. h
8. j
9. c
10. e

QUICK QUIZ 13

1. e
2. d
3. g
4. c
5. a
6. b
7. i
8. h
9. j
10. f

QUICK QUIZ 14

1. e
2. h
3. c
4. g
5. f
6. b
7. a
8. j
9. d
10. i

QUICK QUIZ 15

1. i
2. d
3. h
4. b
5. c
6. a
7. f
8. j
9. e
10. g

QUICK QUIZ 16

1. i
2. g
3. a
4. j
5. b
6. e
7. c
8. h
9. d
10. f

QUICK QUIZ 17

1. c
2. e
3. f
4. g
5. h
6. i
7. b
8. j
9. a
10. d

QUICK QUIZ 18

1. f
2. a
3. g
4. c
5. h
6. i
7. j
8. b
9. d
10. e

QUICK QUIZ 19

1. a
2. b
3. g
4. h
5. i
6. c
7. d
8. f
9. j
10. e

QUICK QUIZ 20

1. d
2. j
3. e
4. h
5. c
6. f
7. g
8. a
9. b
10. i

QUICK QUIZ 21

1. g
2. d
3. j
4. b
5. e
6. a
7. i
8. h
9. c
10. f

QUICK QUIZ 22

1. a
2. e
3. f
4. h
5. i
6. d
7. c
8. g
9. j
10. b

QUICK QUIZ 23

1. d
2. a
3. h
4. c
5. e
6. j
7. i
8. g
9. b
10. f

QUICK QUIZ 24

1. j
2. e
3. g
4. d
5. a
6. h
7. f
8. c
9. b
10. i

QUICK QUIZ 25

1. f
2. e
3. g
4. j
5. h
6. i
7. b
8. d
9. a
10. c

QUICK QUIZ 26

1. i
2. d
3. a
4. e
5. c
6. f
7. j
8. h
9. b
10. g

QUICK QUIZ 27

1. h
2. d
3. j
4. f
5. a
6. i
7. b
8. c
9. g
10. e

QUICK QUIZ 28

1. i
2. j
3. f
4. e
5. d
6. a
7. c
8. b
9. h
10. g

Quick Quiz 29

1. h
2. i
3. d
4. e
5. f
6. c
7. b
8. g
9. a
10. j

Quick Quiz 30

1. d
2. a
3. g
4. j
5. b
6. i
7. f
8. c
9. e
10. h

Quick Quiz 31

1. h
2. g
3. i
4. c
5. f
6. j
7. d
8. b
9. a
10. e

Quick Quiz 32

1. g
2. j
3. b
4. c
5. i
6. e
7. f
8. a
9. d
10. h

Quick Quiz 33

1. g
2. b
3. d
4. f
5. j
6. i
7. e
8. a
9. c
10. h

Quick Quiz 34

1. i
2. h
3. b
4. e
5. c
6. f
7. d
8. j
9. a
10. g

QUICK QUIZ 35

1. i
2. d
3. j
4. h
5. c
6. g
7. f
8. b
9. e
10. a

QUICK QUIZ 36

1. j
2. h
3. d
4. b
5. f
6. g
7. e
8. a
9. i
10. c

QUICK QUIZ 37

1. d
2. b
3. c
4. i
5. f
6. a
7. h
8. g
9. j
10. e

QUICK QUIZ 38

1. d
2. e
3. f
4. g
5. b
6. j
7. h
8. c
9. i
10. a

QUICK QUIZ 39

1. h
2. g
3. f
4. j
5. d
6. i
7. e
8. a
9. c
10. b

QUICK QUIZ 40

1. g
2. e
3. j
4. a
5. i
6. c
7. h
8. f
9. b
10. d

Quick Quiz 41

1. i
2. h
3. b
4. g
5. a
6. c
7. j
8. f
9. d
10. e

Quick Quiz 42

1. h
2. i
3. c
4. f
5. d
6. b
7. a
8. g
9. e
10. j

Quick Quiz 43

1. h
2. b
3. j
4. c
5. f
6. d
7. i
8. e
9. g
10. a

Quick Quiz 44

1. g
2. i
3. d
4. f
5. e
6. a
7. b
8. h
9. c
10. j

Quick Quiz 45

1. h
2. d
3. b
4. j
5. e
6. i
7. f
8. g
9. c
10. a

Quick Quiz 46

1. h
2. e
3. g
4. i
5. f
6. a
7. b
8. d
9. c
10. j

QUICK QUIZ 47

1. a
2. j
3. f
4. b
5. d
6. h
7. g
8. e
9. c
10. i

QUICK QUIZ 48

1. f
2. e
3. g
4. b
5. h
6. c
7. a
8. i
9. d
10. j

QUICK QUIZ 49

1. b
2. j
3. d
4. g
5. f
6. a
7. i
8. c
9. h
10. e

QUICK QUIZ 50

1. h
2. g
3. a
4. f
5. d
6. j
7. b
8. c
9. e
10. i

QUICK QUIZ 51

1. i
2. j
3. e
4. c
5. b
6. f
7. g
8. d
9. a
10. h

QUICK QUIZ 52

1. h
2. f
3. b
4. i
5. d
6. g
7. j
8. c
9. e
10. a

QUICK QUIZ 53

1. c
2. e
3. d
4. a
5. f
6. h
7. i
8. b
9. j
10. g

QUICK QUIZ 54

1. c
2. b
3. d
4. i
5. f
6. e
7. j
8. a
9. g
10. h

QUICK QUIZ 55

1. d
2. a
3. c
4. e
5. i
6. b
7. j
8. g
9. h
10. f

QUICK QUIZ 56

1. i
2. h
3. a
4. c
5. j
6. g
7. e
8. b
9. f
10. d

QUICK QUIZ 57

1. d
2. a
3. j
4. f
5. i
6. g
7. h
8. c
9. b
10. e

QUICK QUIZ 58

1. e
2. j
3. b
4. f
5. c
6. a
7. g
8. h
9. i
10. d

Quick Quiz 59

1. b
2. a
3. f
4. c
5. h
6. d
7. g
8. e
9. j
10. i

Quick Quiz 60

1. g
2. h
3. j
4. c
5. d
6. b
7. i
8. a
9. e
10. f

Quick Quiz 61

1. a
2. g
3. c
4. j
5. f
6. i
7. e
8. d
9. h
10. b

Quick Quiz 62

1. c
2. h
3. f
4. b
5. i
6. e
7. d
8. g
9. j
10. a

Quick Quiz 63

1. j
2. d
3. g
4. i
5. a
6. c
7. e
8. b
9. h
10. f

Quick Quiz 64

1. e
2. g
3. c
4. i
5. h
6. f
7. d
8. j
9. b
10. a

QUICK QUIZ 65

1. c
2. g
3. b
4. d
5. e
6. f
7. a

FINAL EXAM DRILL 1

1. f
2. b
3. g
4. h
5. a
6. c
7. j
8. d
9. i
10. e

FINAL EXAM DRILL 2

1. d
2. k
3. a
4. c
5. l
6. f
7. h
8. e
9. j
10. g
11. i
12. b

FINAL EXAM DRILL 3

1. f
2. e
3. a
4. c
5. d
6. j
7. g
8. h
9. b
10. i

FINAL EXAM DRILL 4

1. g
2. h
3. m
4. l
5. d
6. f
7. i
8. k
9. b
10. a
11. e
12. c
13. j

FINAL EXAM DRILL 5

1. c
2. e
3. i
4. g
5. a
6. f
7. h
8. d
9. b
10. j

Final Exam Drill 6

1. j
2. h
3. g
4. i
5. c
6. f
7. e
8. b
9. d
10. a

Final Exam Drill 7

1. d
2. f
3. g
4. e
5. h
6. c
7. b
8. j
9. a
10. i

Final Exam Drill 8

1. h
2. f
3. a
4. j
5. g
6. c
7. b
8. d
9. i
10. e

Final Exam Drill 9

1. g
2. i
3. f
4. c
5. e
6. b
7. a
8. h
9. j
10. d

Final Exam Drill 10

1. h
2. c
3. g
4. a
5. f
6. d
7. b
8. i
9. j
10. e

Final Exam Drill 11

1. f
2. a
3. e
4. d
5. i
6. g
7. b
8. c
9. j
10. h

FINAL EXAM DRILL 12

1. g
2. f
3. e
4. c
5. a
6. i
7. d
8. h
9. b
10. j

FINAL EXAM DRILL 13

1. b
2. b
3. b
4. a
5. b
6. a
7. a
8. b
9. b
10. a

FINAL EXAM DRILL 14

1. j
2. f
3. g
4. e
5. i
6. c
7. h
8. a
9. b
10. d

FINAL EXAM DRILL 15

1. c
2. i
3. h
4. b
5. d
6. j
7. f
8. g
9. a
10. e

FINAL EXAM DRILL 16

1. b
2. c
3. a
4. i
5. d
6. g
7. e
8. f
9. h
10. j

FINAL EXAM DRILL 17

1. c
2. g
3. f
4. j
5. b
6. h
7. a
8. i
9. d
10. e

Final Exam Drill 18

1. d
2. i
3. b
4. j
5. a
6. h
7. c
8. e
9. f
10. g

Final Exam Drill 19

1. b
2. a
3. b
4. b
5. b
6. b
7. b
8. b
9. b
10. b

Final Exam Drill 20

1. a
2. d
3. j
4. e
5. c
6. f
7. i
8. b
9. g
10. h

Final Exam Drill 21

1. c
2. d
3. a
4. h
5. b
6. g
7. e
8. i
9. j
10. f

Final Exam Drill 22

1. b
2. f
3. j
4. a
5. i
6. e
7. h
8. d
9. c
10. g

Final Exam Drill 23

1. b
2. d
3. f
4. g
5. i
6. c
7. e
8. a
9. j
10. h

FINAL EXAM DRILL 24

1. b
2. b
3. b
4. b
5. a
6. b
7. b
8. a
9. a
10. a

FINAL EXAM DRILL 25

1. b
2. j
3. d
4. f
5. a
6. g
7. e
8. h
9. c
10. i

FINAL EXAM DRILL 26

1. b
2. f
3. e
4. j
5. d
6. c
7. h
8. a
9. i
10. g

FINAL EXAM DRILL 27

1. f
2. c
3. j
4. b
5. e
6. a
7. i
8. h
9. d
10. g

FINAL EXAM DRILL 28

1. j
2. b
3. a
4. h
5. i
6. f
7. c
8. e
9. d
10. g

FINAL EXAM DRILL 29

1. g
2. j
3. e
4. b
5. a
6. i
7. c
8. h
9. d
10. f

FINAL EXAM DRILL 30

1. d
2. h
3. a
4. f
5. i
6. b
7. e
8. c
9. g
10. j

FINAL EXAM DRILL 31

1. g
2. h
3. j
4. b
5. f
6. c
7. d
8. i
9. e
10. a

FINAL EXAM DRILL 32

1. b
2. a
3. a
4. b
5. a
6. b
7. a
8. b
9. b
10. b

FINAL EXAM DRILL 33

1. e
2. j
3. b
4. i
5. h
6. a
7. d
8. f
9. g
10. c

FINAL EXAM DRILL 34

1. h
2. f
3. i
4. b
5. a
6. g
7. c
8. e
9. j
10. d

FINAL EXAM DRILL 35

1. i
2. c
3. e
4. f
5. j
6. g
7. b
8. a
9. d
10. h

FINAL EXAM DRILL 36

1. b
2. b
3. b
4. a
5. b
6. b
7. a
8. b
9. a
10. b

FINAL EXAM DRILL 37

1. h
2. f
3. a
4. b
5. e
6. d
7. i
8. c
9. j
10. g

FINAL EXAM DRILL 38

1. e
2. g
3. h
4. c
5. f
6. a
7. j
8. i
9. d
10. b

FINAL EXAM DRILL 39

1. e
2. a
3. c
4. b
5. d
6. j
7. i
8. g
9. f
10. h

FINAL EXAM DRILL 40

1. i
2. b
3. h
4. f
5. c
6. a
7. e
8. g
9. d
10. j

FINAL EXAM DRILL 41

1. b
2. a
3. b
4. a
5. a
6. b
7. b
8. b
9. a
10. b

FINAL EXAM DRILL 42

1. f
2. d
3. a
4. h
5. e
6. g
7. b
8. c
9. j
10. i

FINAL EXAM DRILL 43

1. j
2. d
3. i
4. e
5. f
6. b
7. c
8. h
9. g
10. a

FINAL EXAM DRILL 44

1. a
2. a
3. a
4. a
5. a
6. b
7. a
8. a
9. a
10. b

FINAL EXAM DRILL 45

1. b
2. e
3. j
4. a
5. g
6. i
7. d
8. c
9. h
10. f

FINAL EXAM DRILL 46

1. i
2. j
3. g
4. h
5. a
6. e
7. b
8. f
9. c
10. d

FINAL EXAM DRILL 47

1. f
2. h
3. b
4. j
5. e
6. i
7. d
8. g
9. a
10. c

FINAL EXAM DRILL 48

1. a
2. g
3. c
4. f
5. i
6. d
7. j
8. e
9. h
10. b

FINAL EXAM DRILL 49

1. a
2. a
3. b
4. b
5. a
6. b
7. b
8. a
9. a
10. a

FINAL EXAM DRILL 50

1. c
2. j
3. a
4. g
5. f
6. e
7. d
8. h
9. i
10. b

FINAL EXAM DRILL 51

1. d
2. g
3. h
4. b
5. i
6. f
7. e
8. a
9. c
10. j

FINAL EXAM DRILL 52

1. a
2. g
3. h
4. i
5. c
6. f
7. j
8. b
9. e
10. d

FINAL EXAM DRILL 53

1. i
2. h
3. j
4. c
5. e
6. a
7. b
8. d
9. f
10. g

Final Exam Drill 54

1. i
2. c
3. h
4. g
5. e
6. j
7. d
8. b
9. a
10. f

Final Exam Drill 55

1. h
2. e
3. d
4. a
5. i
6. g
7. b
8. f
9. j
10. c

Final Exam Drill 56

1. g
2. h
3. a
4. e
5. i
6. f
7. j
8. c
9. b
10. d

Final Exam Drill 57

1. i
2. j
3. b
4. g
5. c
6. h
7. a
8. e
9. d
10. f

ABOUT THE AUTHOR

Michael Freedman has written and taught for The Princeton Review for many years. Michael lives in Brooklyn with two cats, his wife Grace, and their brand new son, Jacob. This is his second book for The Princeton Review.